LIVING TO

PLEASE GOD

LIVING TO PLEASE GOD

Following the example of Jesus

David Haag

Christian Focus Publications

©1992 David Haag

ISBN 0 906 731 91 7

Published by
Christian Focus Publications Ltd
Geanies House, Fearn, Ross-shire,
IV20 1TW, Scotland, Great Britain.

Scripture quotations are from
the New King James Version.

Cover design
by
Donna Macleod

Printed and bound in Great Britain by
Cox & Wyman Ltd, Reading

CONTENTS

To
Annette,
my wife and friend,
and our children,
Laura, Nathan, Heather and Andrea.

To eat, to breathe
to beget
Is this all there is
Chance configuration of atom against atom
    of god against god
I cannot believe it.

Come, Christian Triune God who lives,
Here am I
Shake the world again.

Francis A. Schaeffer 1912-1984

FOREWORD

This is a valuable book. It is no sterile, dry-as-dust tome. Could it be otherwise when it considers the greatest life ever lived?

Dr Haag selects significant events and periods from the life of Christ and applies these to our own. It is intellectually stimulating, biblically enriching, theologically sound and spiritually challenging.

Everywhere there is evidence of penetrating biblical investigation where doctrine and duty, belief and behaviour are joined together. The thoughtful theologian blends beautifully with the practical Bible teacher as the great spiritual issues are faced. Biblical theology properly presented is never dull or uninteresting. It is vital, penetrating, confrontational, for we come face to face with God in Christ, and that is thrilling, humbling and life-transforming. There is a wide range of theological thought in the numerous quotations, as we hear from W E Vine, A W Tozer, Francis Schaeffer, C S Lewis and many others. Scholarship is mingled with down-to-earth practical challenge as David Haag argues from a strong biblical base.

He speaks of 'the radical teaching of Christ's example which breaks into our lives and compels us to consider Him'. And consider Him we do. From the truth of God incarnate, through the remarkable lessons learned from His hidden years, His dedication to God's purpose at His baptism, His temptation, so full of instruction, to His marvellous teaching, particularly that of His attitude to the Scriptures, His teaching about Himself, the Holy Spirit, sin and salvation. We read of Christ the Servant, serving in the power of the Holy Spirit, in humility, in compassion. 'Serving God the Father cost the Son everything. We should ask ourselves, What is it costing me to serve Him?'

Then there is His prayer-life, detailed and dynamic.

This rich revelation culminates in the great event of the cross of Calvary. 'If we are to live in Christ and He in us, we must first die with Him. This is the basis of the true Christian life,' says David Haag. The mighty work of the cross is applied personally. The cross means self-denial, sacrifice, crucifixion. To pass this way through faith is to lead to the resurrection, where we find power 'not only to rise again, but to live in the glory of the resurrection in the present'.

Considering Him, trusting in Him day after day, should bring conformity to Him - and that is what this book is really all about.

May many receive its message and be transformed by considering in faith the greatest life ever lived.

Colin N. Peckham
BA (Hons), BTh; MTh

But he who would fully and with true relish understand the words of Christ, must study to make his whole life conformable to that of Christ.

Thomas a Kempis *The Imitation of Christ*

God's highest purpose in the redemption of sinful humanity was based in His hope that we would allow Him to reproduce the likeness of Jesus Christ in our once sinful lives.

A. W. Tozer *Who Put Jesus on the Cross*

We are to love God, we are to be alive to him, we are to be in communion with him, in this present moment in history.

Francis A. Schaeffer *True Spirituality*

INTRODUCTION

By the end of the twentieth century, an estimated forty billion people will have lived upon the earth. Among all of these billions of people there is a single central individual, the one most important person the world will ever know, Jesus Christ, the Son of God.

His life on the earth covered about thirty-three years and was remarkable in its similarity to the lives of His contemporaries. Christ's death on the cross of Calvary took about six hours and was a death like no other. While it may be said that Christ came to earth to die for mankind, it is also true that the life He lived prior to His death was of great significance and benefit, for the Christian life is based upon both the life and death of Jesus Christ. In His death is the source of our eternal, spiritual life, and in the life He lived is the pattern to which this new life is to conform. As Hebrews 12:2 states, He is both the Author and the Finisher of our faith. And the Apostle Paul's observation in Colossians 2:10, that we are 'complete in Him' is based upon the benefits which are ours through Christ's life and death.

In each of the four Gospels we are given an account of events in Christ's life. While they do not constitute a biography, they do provide an inspired record of His time on earth. From them we learn what we *need* to know about His life, if not all we may *want* to know. Throughout the New Testament we are frequently told that our lives as Christians are to be lived after Christ's example. Paul especially reminds us that it is Christ who is living 'in us', and that we are to walk as He walked. Peter states very plainly that Christ's life is to be our example and that we are to follow in His steps (1 Peter 2:21). His steps lead eventually to the cross, but before bringing Him to that destination they take Him through territory traversed by all of us during our earthly life. Christ was a member of a family, He lived and worked among others in society, He experienced temptation as all men do and through all of this He maintained a personal relationship with the Father through His Word and prayer, carrying out a specific ministry which was God's will for His life.

Christ tells us that if we are to find rest for our own souls, we must take on His yoke and learn of Him (Matthew 11:29-30). His yoke and our cross belong to our earthly life and are to be borne after His example. They are to be carried as we place our feet in the prints He has left for us to follow.

Perhaps more books have been written about the life of Christ than about any other individual. Through the centuries the minds of many have been captivated by Him, whether from an historical or Christian perspective. Although much has already been written there is no life more deserving of our attention than His.

Early in the fifteenth century, during one of the darkest periods of Christian history, a book entitled *The Imitation of Christ* was written. Its author is generally believed to have been a German mystic, Thomas a Kempis of Cologne. Although tinged with superstition and bearing the influence of the monasticism of its author, it is a remarkable book, casting considerable light in a particularly dark era.

Throughout this book Thomas calls the reader to Christ-likeness, as the title suggests, through the imitation of His life. Care must be taken in the interpretation of this call for it is not in our power to be like Christ simply by trying to imitate Him. It is important to note that imitation does not make us sons of God, but sonship is the true starting point for a Christ-like life. Having begun here by God's grace, we proceed in the development of our Christian life by His grace as well. The power to do so is given to us as part of the great gift of salvation. When we receive Christ as Saviour He comes to live within us in the person of the Holy Spirit.

12

The ability to follow Christ is ours only as the Spirit of God is in us and living through us.

Although flawed, Thomas' *Imitation of Christ* has been a stimulus to Christian living for many since its publication in the fifteenth century. Another book developing the same theme but following a different approach was written by a Scotsman, Professor James Stalker, late in the nineteenth century. In the introduction to his *Imago Christi* he points out that during the preceding century the Modernists had stressed Christ's humanity, making much of the value of His example, and the Evangelicals had stressed Christ's divinity and the value of His atonement. Stalker objected to this division, pointing out that Christ is both fully God and fully man, divine and human. In this rests His uniqueness and virtue. Professor Stalker wrote:

> 'The death of Christ is ours, and we rest in it our hopes of acceptance with God in time and in eternity. This is what we begin with; but we do not end with it. We will go on from His death to His life and, with the love begotten of being redeemed, try to reproduce that life in our own. In the same way, whilst glorying in His divinity, we will allow none to rob us of the attraction and the example of His humanity; for, indeed, the perfection of His humanity, with what this implies as to the value of His testimony about himself, is the strongest bulwark of our faith that He was more than man.'[1]

It is with this in mind that we consider the life of Jesus Christ as found in Scripture and as it applies to our own Christian lives. Today, when Christ is spoken of it is often as a *man*, seldom as a the *God-man*. The reality of His divinity is that it was lived in His humanity. Christians witness that He is God today as He lives His life within their humanity. Christ living in them is not only their hope of glory, but, as He is seen in them, it may be the hope of glory for those around them as well.

The image of God
The answer to the Psalmist's question, 'What is man that You are mindful of him, and the son of man that You visit him?' (Psalm 8:4),

is the theme of the Bible. God thinks of man because man alone, of all His creation, is made in His image. He visited us because He loved us, even though we are separated from Him by our sins. Man, God's creation, is loved by God, who has a purpose for him.

Man, made in the image of God, is linked to God from creation, similar to Him, yet different; not divine, but dependent on Him. As God is eternal, He gave man an immortal soul. As God is a personal God, He gave us our personalities, characterized by the abilities of self-consciousness and moral responsibility. To man is given intelligence, sensitive to the beauty of His creation about us and having the capacity to recognize our own complex emotions within. And, as God is Spirit, He made man spiritual beings, able to love and worship Him, and to enjoy fellowship with Him. Also, and very importantly, He made man holy.

The first two chapters of Genesis tell of man's creation and life in the beauty and perfection of Eden. Chapter 3 describes the record of man's temptation, fall and the entrance of sin into the human experience. In many ways this third chapter is central to all of God's message in Scripture. If we do not understand its meaning and the implications of what it contains we can never understand ourselves nor our world.

Man's life in Eden before the fall was a delight in every way. Then his conscious awareness of God was complete and he viewed everything in life in relation to Him. God was the focal point, giving meaning and direction to himself and all else. Before the fall, man recognized the will of God and submitted to it freely. Because of this relationship, there was communion involving the natural and free interaction of man and his Creator. And man was alive! Fully alive in both the physical and spiritual dimensions of life as established by God. There existed neither physical death, the separation of the soul from the body, nor spiritual death, the separation of the soul from God. Eden was a place of perfection and man was its perfect inhabitant, and presumably man would have continued to live forever in this condition had it not been for the fall.

As an historical event the fall occurred when first Eve, and then

Adam was tempted. Their temptation was based upon a choice - the truth of God, or the lie of Satan. The choice they made produced the actions and consequences which followed. Having chosen to reject God's rule, their lives were altered immediately, and through them, less immediately but just as certainly, our lives and world were changed as well. It is this universal nature of the fall that Paul points out in Romans 5:12 when he explains that 'just as through one man sin entered the world, and death through sin, and thus death spread to all men, because all sinned'.

The life into which men are born after the fall is very different from that of Adam and Eve. No longer are their lives focused on God nor is life in general seen in relation to Him. The shift from God to self is universal; by nature, it is our will and not the will of God which rules. God, our Divine centre, is denied, and with this the meaning and direction of life is lost. In our lost condition there is no longer the spontaneous communication once shared with God as in Eden. In its place there is now guilt, shame and fear. The difference between life before and after the fall is as great as that between light and darkness. Man is no longer holy, and he no longer seeks God. God's image in man is marred and cannot be restored even by our best efforts.

Reading the first three chapters of Genesis it might seem that God's purpose for us has been completely destroyed by the fall. Yet, as sad as this message is and as dark as man's plight seems, there is still the offer of light and hope. Genesis 3:15 is a combined promise and prophecy as God announces His judgment on Satan and promises deliverance for mankind: 'I will put enmity between you and the woman, and between your seed and her Seed; He shall bruise your head, and you shall bruise His heel.'

The *Seed* God promises here is Jesus Christ, who would come to deliver us. He will be born as one of us; he will be tempted as all men are; He will live as we live; yet by His life, He will light our way out of eternal darkness. It is Christ who is the subject of Old Testament prophecy and New Testament fulfilment. What God achieves through Him will make possible the realization of His purpose for mankind.

When men receive Christ as Saviour they are then 'hidden with (Him) in God' (Col 3:3). Through Christ the union between man and God which existed before the fall is restored and men begin to learn that in Jesus' life and death there is both the example and possibility for their holiness, the restoration of God's image in them. Christians are *complete* in Christ (Colossians 2:10); and they are given 'all things that pertain to life and godliness' (2 Peter 1:3). Therein lies their security and hope for life in time and eternity.

In coming to live on earth in His incarnation, Christ fulfilled a two-fold purpose. (i) By His death He bore the penalty of our sins and became our Saviour, securing our place in heaven. (ii) By His life He provided us a perfect example to follow as we live our lives here on earth. In his letters, Paul explains the meaning of this two-fold purpose as it relates to ourselves. Our relationship with Christ must begin with death before it can proceed to life. Using the image of baptism he says, 'we were buried with Him through baptism into death, that just as Christ was raised from the dead by the glory of the Father, even so we also should walk in newness of life' (Romans 6:4). It is first death and then life. Paul uses the terms *old* and *new* man to signify our life before and after salvation. It is our old man which must be put to death with Christ on the cross, and along with it our natural inclinations to sin and this world (Galatians 6:14; Romans 6:11). With the death of the old man there is the birth of the new, resurrected from death as Christ was, and walking in newness of life. Our new life is different in every way from the old, and is characterized by supernatural inclinations toward God and heavenly things.

What was lost universally in the fall, God begins to restore individually to us. The results of our salvation flow through all of our new life in Christ as God continues to work in our lives through His Spirit, conforming us to the image of His Son. This work continues till the end of our earthly life, culminating in eternity, when we shall appear in His likeness (Psalm 17:15). In Galatians 2:20, Paul further explains our transition from death to life and our transformation from life centred in self to a life centred in Christ. His testimony describes our own experience: 'I have been crucified with Christ; it is no longer I who live, but Christ lives in me; and the life which I now live in the flesh I live by faith in the Son of God, who loved me and gave Himself for me.'

This verse contains four themes, each of which is linked to the one preceding, and all of which, when taken together, present a clear statement of the two-fold purpose of Christ's life in relation to our own.

(a) 'I have been crucified with Christ.' When Paul refers to death, he is describing our identification by faith with Christ crucified. It is at this point that our spiritual life has its beginning.

(b) 'It is no longer I who live, but Christ lives in me.' Next he refers to, what he calls elsewhere, a 'mystery', Christ living in us (Col 1:27). It is this mystery which Christ, in picture form, explains through the analogy of the Vine and branches in John 15. There He identifies Himself as the Vine, with believers as the branches, and declares that the life of the Vine becomes the life of the branches. From John 14:16-20, we learn that the way He lives in us is through the Holy Spirit who indwells us, having been sent by the Father on behalf of the Son.

(c) 'The life which I now live in the flesh.' Here Paul makes an important statement about an aspect of our new life - that it is lived 'in the flesh', in our body, on the earth. Through His death Christ secures eternity for us, but this is not the only dimension of His concern and provision, for in the most personal way He involves Himself in our life in time, as day by day we approach eternity.

(d) 'The life which I now live in the flesh, I live by faith in the Son of God.' Finally, Paul declares that our new life is to be a life of faith. This is the defining principle of the true Christian life, for without faith, it can neither begin nor continue. And the distinctive of this faith is its object, Jesus Christ.

1 Peter 2:21 says that Christ is our example. The Greek word Peter uses for 'example' means literally an 'under-writing' and implies an exact copy that is given to a student for reproduction as he lays his own paper over it and traces the original. Christ's life, as found in the Bible is the 'under-writing' over which we are to place our own lives, allowing the Original to be reproduced in us.[2]

Paul follows a similar line of thinking when he says that 'we all, with unveiled face, behold as in a mirror the glory of the Lord, are being transformed into the same image from glory to glory, just as by the Spirit of the Lord' (2 Cor 3:18). As Peter stresses Christ as our example, Paul stresses the Holy Spirit as our Helper in following His example.

Peter also tells us that to follow Christ's example is to walk in His steps. The following chapters are designed to help us see the footprints of Christ as He walked on earth in life-situations similar to our own.

One of God's great purposes for Christians is that we should be holy. Our holiness increases as our conformity to Christ increases, for following in the footsteps of Christ fulfils God's purpose in our lives. As it is fulfilled in us, it may be fulfilled in others, as they see Christ in our lives and are drawn to Him.

References

1. James Stalker, *Imago Christi*, London: Hodder and Stoughton, 1895, p.33.
2. R C H Lenski, *The Interpretation of the Epistles of St Peter, St John and St Jude*, Columbus, Ohio: Wartburg Press, 1945, pp. 119, 120.

The Word became flesh. The statement is appalling, overwhelming. Out of the infinite distances, into the finite nearness; from the unknowable, to the knowable; from the method of self-expression appreciable by Deity alone, to a method of self-expression understandable of the human.

G. Campbell Morgan, *The Crises of the Christ*

If you want to get the hang of it, think how you would like to become a slug or a crab.

C. S. Lewis, *Mere Christianity*

The Word of God, Jesus Christ, on account of His great love for mankind, became what we are in order to make us what He is himself.

Irenaeus

Behold, a virgin shall be with child, and bear a Son, and they shall call His name Immanuel, which is translated, God with us.

Matthew 1:23

1

THE INCARNATION

In the introduction we examined Christ's coming in relation to its two-fold purpose: to secure our salvation by His death, and, through His life, to present an example of how we should live. In this chapter we turn to one of the most important doctrines in the Bible, the incarnation. This doctrine involves God becoming man, yet retaining all of His qualities as God while living on earth in the Person of Jesus Christ.

Doctrine defined

That Jesus was both God and man at the same time is a foundational tenet of Scripture and has been widely accepted throughout the history of the Christian Church. This was the issue dealt with by the Council of Chalcedon in 451 AD which affirmed that Christ was 'complete in Godhead and complete in manhood, truly God and truly man, having two natures, without confusion, without change, without division, without separation. That these two natures came together in complete harmony in the one Person of Jesus Christ has been the orthodox view of Christ since the fifth century'.[1]

Incarnation - the God-Man

Although the word incarnation is not found in the Bible its component parts, in carne (in flesh) are found in several places. In

1 Timothy 3:16 Paul expresses its meaning as God 'manifested in the flesh', and he describes this manifestation in Romans 8:3 as the act of God sending 'His own Son in the likeness of sinful flesh'. Peter adds that this ultimately resulted in Christ both 'suffering for us in the flesh' and 'being put to death in the flesh'. (1 Peter 4:l; 3:18)

Although Christ's coming in this manner was initiated at His conception, His incarnation should not be regarded as simply that brief act by which He entered human life. Rather it encompasses all of His life as Professor Thomas Torrence explains in this statement.

> 'By the incarnation Christian theology means that at a definite point in space and time the Son of God became man, born at Bethlehem of Mary, a virgin espoused to a man called Joseph, a Jew of the tribe and lineage of David, and towards the end of the reign of Herod the Great in Judea. Given the name of Jesus, He fulfilled His mission from the Father, living out the span of earthly life allotted to Him until He was crucified under Pontius Pilate, but when after three days He rose again from the dead the eyes of Jesus' disciples were opened to what it all meant: they knew Him to be God's Son, declared with power and installed in Messianic Office, and so they went out to proclaim Him to all nations as the Lord and Saviour of the world. Thus it is the faith and understanding of the Christian Church that in Jesus Christ God Himself in His own flesh has come into our world and is actively present as personal Agent within our physical and historical existence.'[2]

The incarnation and its implications are the basis of many New Testament passages and one of its clearest statements is found in the Prologue of John's Gospel. In verse 14 he writes that 'the Word became flesh and dwelt among us, and we beheld His glory, the glory as of the only begotten of the Father, full of grace and truth'. When John says that the Word became flesh, he does not mean merely that He entered into a human body as we might place our hand into a glove. It was much more than this, for in our analogy the hand and the glove, though closely joined, continue to have wholly separate identities and are independent of each other. John does not say that Christ *took* a body - as a hand might take a glove upon itself.

Rather, while retaining His divine nature, He assumed a complete human nature and became a completely unique being, the God-man. The commentator Godet makes a helpful observation on what takes place as he says, 'It designates the *reality* and *integrity* of the human mode of existence into which Jesus entered. In virtue of this incarnation, He was able to suffer, to enjoy, to be tempted, to struggle, to learn, to make progress, to love, to pray, exactly *like us*'.[3]

There are definitely some dimensions of the incarnation we cannot understand - that is how it is with God. So long as we remember this we are on the pathway to greater understanding. Knowing Him and His ways is a step-by-step walk of faith that is based upon revelation. We should remember that all of the Bible is God's revelation, in that it discloses truth about God and His plan. Our focus should be on what we can understand rather than what we cannot. What we can understand of the incarnation forms the basis for going on to greater understanding of this mystery. We certainly should know this: God, who is Spirit and invisible, became visible flesh through an act of great condescension.

Professor Torrence has described the incarnation as an 'utterly staggering' doctrine. It appears this way to men because what it teaches is completely outside of anything that can be experienced by man. Because of this it has been a point of dispute between orthodoxy and unorthodoxy for centuries. There have always been, as there are today, those who have tried to remove it from the fundamental requirements of the Christian faith. Their attempts to produce a Christianity without the incarnation have resulted in a non-supernatural faith lacking in both truth and power and denying the very Word of God by which we come to know of this doctrine.

Who is He?

Historically there have been three conclusions drawn by men as they have considered the Person of Jesus Christ: (i) He is God, (ii) He is man, (iii) He is both God and man. It is the last of these which is taught by Christ himself in Scripture: 'I and My Father are one

... The Father is in Me and I in Him' (John 10:30, 38). This unity was true before, during and after the incarnation, and to turn aside from this belief is to enter into the most dangerous form of heresy. In his Epistles John stresses the fundamental necessity of adhering to this doctrine. He warns that 'many deceivers have gone out into the world who do not confess Jesus Christ as coming in the flesh. This is a deceiver and an antichrist' (2 John 7). Some of the New Testament's strongest condemnation is directed at those who deny this truth.

Men of every generation have been fascinated with Jesus, but sadly in our own time much of the attention focused on His life and ministry, has been extremely critical. In the sixties the theology of *The Death of God* emerged declaring that Jesus was only a *name* and not a *Person*, and that there had been no real incarnation at all. The consequence of such belief is that we are left alone in the universe, neither ruled nor loved by God. Therefore, there is no God to save or guide, He never became man to live among us, there is only man.

Although this teaching has died a theological death it continues to have an influence in other forms. It made a significant contribution to the secularisation of Christianity in the seventies and eighties. During this era of secularisation a group of theologians in England published a book entitled *The Myth of God Incarnate* in which they argue against an actual, historical, supernatural entrance by God into our world. The following paragraph is from the second chapter of this book and was written by Francis Young of Birmingham University.

'The Christians of the early church lived in a world in which supernatural visitants were not unexpected. Such assumptions, however, have become foreign to our own situation. In the Western world, both popular culture and the culture of the intelligentsia has come to be dominated by the human and natural sciences to such an extent that supernatural causation or intervention in the affairs of this world has become, for the majority of people, simply incredible ... History is to be explained in terms of politics and personalities, or economics and power structures. Heavenly powers have given way to earthly forces.'[4]

It is open to question whether, as Young says, the majority have turned to earthly forces rather than heavenly powers to explain what is. Certainly some have, yet just as certainly a great many have not, and for them the Bible, and all the supernaturalism it contains, is the truth that matters, and the Christ whose life it reveals is relevant to all of contemporary life.

No doubt the incarnation has been the target of such consistent attack over the centuries because of its importance to the Christian Faith. Remove it and the whole of Christianity falls. For if God did not become man just as Scripture says, then there is neither salvation nor a divine pattern for our lives. Effectively God would then be dead to man, there would have been no past contact between the Divine and the human, and there could be none in the present. Man would be left alone on the earth.

A practical doctrine

Although the incarnation is mysterious, it is presented to us in the form most easily understood, that of the life of Jesus Christ. It must be taken finally by faith but it isn't faith without any foundation in reality. As C. S. Lewis has written, 'If a myth had become fact, had been incarnated, it would be just like this.'[5] This doctrine has the ring of truth about it in the human heart.

The incarnation is eminently practical. In the Gospels we observe the thoughts and actions of our example, Jesus Christ. We are shown that God meets us where we are and communicates a way of living to us far more relevant and applicable than even the most elaborate system of ethics.

The parallel between our spiritual life and the life of Christ begins with birth, His physical birth and our spiritual birth. As God, Christ is eternal, therefore His existence did not begin at His conception. However, that was the way by which the eternal merged with the temporal and God began life on earth as man. Although there is no similarity between our life and the eternal existence of Christ, in a different sense we too have life before our spiritual birth in that we are alive physically. But it is only at conversion that we become fully alive, both physically and spiritually, and begin to experience life as created and intended by God. It is at this point that the pattern of life revealed in Christ's physical life must be brought to bear upon our own. However, the practicality of the incarnation lies not only in the earthly life it enabled Christ to live before a watching world, but in the actual process of His becoming man. Inherent in this are all the lessons He lived out during His thirty-three or so years. Therefore, before we look at other areas of His life, we will first look carefully at what was involved in the actual process of His coming down from heaven, for that is where it all begins.

Why did God become Man?

God never does anything without purpose and for our study we will consider a two-fold purpose for the incarnation.

First, Christ came to reveal God to mankind. What better way could there be for us to know what God is like than by having Him come to live as one of us, among us. And what could be more plain and practical than for Him, having done so, then to say, 'Follow in My footsteps'?

Secondly, Christ came to reconcile men to the Father. Reconciliation is basic to His coming and the way God chose to accomplish it required the incarnation. In Galatians 4:4 Paul tells us that Christ was born at God's appointed time, that He was born of a woman and under the rule of the law. During His lifetime He fulfilled the law, meeting all of its demands and more:

> 'For what the law could not do in that it was weak through the flesh, God did by sending His own Son in the likeness of sinful flesh, on account of sin: He condemned sin in the flesh' (Rom. 8:3).

The cause of our separation from God is sin and our hope for reconciliation is Christ. And this is accomplished by God through the incarnation as He 'was in Christ reconciling the world to Himself' (2 Cor. 5:19).

With these purposes in mind let us consider their application to ourselves. As Christ was born to reveal God to others, so we are born again for this same purpose. In John 9:5 Christ says, 'As long as I am in the world, I am the light of the world.' However, when He withdrew His physical presence from the world at His ascension, light was still needed.

This continuing need is to be met by the Christian for we are the light of the world. Men are to see our lives, our good works, and glorify our Father in heaven (Matt. 5:14,16). Following the resurrection Christ lives in every believer in the Person of the Holy Spirit. Thus it is His life and light revealed through believers that illuminates the darkness of every age, showing men the way to God. And the more closely we become conformed to Christ's image, the more clearly He will be revealed in us before our contemporaries.

Following from this base is our effectiveness in reconciliation, Christ's second purpose in coming. While this is ultimately the work of God, we too have a part in it. As God was in Christ reconciling the world to Himself, so Christ is in us, involving us in the ministry of reconciliation, making us His ambassadors and pleading through us with others to come to Him (2 Cor. 5:18-20). These two purposes were brought together perfectly in Christ and as they become integral parts of our spiritual lives they link us with God's great plan, and involve us in its fulfilment as Christ extends His ministry through us.

Now, having looked at these purposes and their applications, we are ready to consider other aspects of His example revealed in the act of incarnation. In order to do this we turn to one of the most important New Testament passages relating to this doctrine, Philippians 2:5-8. Here Paul traces Christ's downward progression from His form as God to His assumption of the form of a servant, His appearance as man and obedience to death by crucifixion.

One of the most striking things about this passage is its immediate context. Paul makes his detailed doctrinal statement on the incarnation in a pastoral setting. He presents it as the practical means by which the Philippian believers can resolve the problems of Christian living. If they come to understand and emulate the thoughts and conduct of Christ as exemplified in the incarnation all will be well among them and God will be pleased with their lives.

That all is not well is evident from what Paul says in Philippians 2:2-4. Here he directs our attention to three problem areas in their lives. Really he could be writing of our own generation, or of any for that matter, because the problems he mentions are among those most universal to Christians.

Unity

From verse 2 we learn that their first problem was a lack of unity. Paul says they did not share the same love and were not of one mind. Although he is addressing believers, and as such they were all 'in Christ,' still they were not like-minded. Their thoughts were not in harmony with one another, and more importantly they were not in accord with Christ. And it follows that if they were not agreeing in thought, they could not be united in their conduct as the two are closely joined.

This first problem is the basis for the other two identified in the passage. In verse 3 Paul begins by saying, 'Let nothing be *done...*' What we do is determined by what we think. Therefore in all our thoughts, we must have the mind of Christ. And this is precisely the point at which he begins to develop the doctrine of the incarnation in verse 5. The one-mindedness toward which we are directed is the mind of Christ. All whose thoughts are ruled by His example will be in conformity with Him, and if with Him, then with all who are like-minded. There can be no true unity apart from this conformity to Christ in our thought life.

Humility

Verse 3 introduces the second problem troubling these believers, their lack of humility. Paul points out that their conduct was motivated by selfish ambition and characterized by conceit and self-exaltation. Because they were thinking more highly of themselves than they should, their lives were marked by such unbecoming conduct for Christians. In this verse he uses the phrase 'lowliness of mind'. By this he does not mean that a poor self-image is to be cultivated. They are not to consider themselves as having no worth. Rather he refers to the humility of Christ which characterizes the conduct of those whose thoughts conform to His.

The idea behind the phrase is the conduct Christ exhibited in John 13 as He willingly washed the feet of the disciples, doing the work of the most lowly servant. In that chapter He tells the disciples that He has done this as an example for them to follow. Such a concept is perhaps as contrary as any we could imagine to the natural human spirit, and certainly to the spirit of our own age. It is in such areas as this that Christianity is truly radical, as Christ's example calls us to a way of living so very different from what is the accepted norm for our day.

Selflessness

The third of the Philippians' problems is found in verse 4. Thinking only of themselves they are forgetting completely those around them. Here the emphasis is on the difference between *selfishness* and *selflessness*. Paul's exhortation to them is that they should be concerned for the interests of others. However, it is interesting to notice that in urging this he says that it can be done while we are also looking out for our own interests. It isn't sinful to have concern for ourselves, Scripture requires this of us. The sin of selfishness emerges when it is *only* ourselves for whom we show concern, to the exclusion of everyone else. In a later chapter we will look at Christ's High Priestly Prayer of Intercession found in John 17. In this model prayer the Lord begins by praying for Himself. This is the focus of the first five verses, and only after having prayed for Himself does He turn His attention toward others.

The three problems present in the Philippian Church are all interrelated. Thinking only of themselves is an expected consequence of a lack of humility. And thinking more highly of themselves than is proper, would not promote an harmonious unity with others. What they needed was a radical change in their thinking. Such a change Paul describes in Romans 12:2 when he writes, 'Do not be conformed to this world, but be transformed by the renewing of your mind, that you may prove what is that good and acceptable and perfect will of God'.

Again we notice in this verse that doing God's will follows from what goes on in the mind. It is the transformation of the mind which breaks our conformity to the world and produces Christ-likeness, first in our thoughts and then in our conduct. Transformation, as Paul uses it here, involves a gradual change brought about by the working of the Holy Spirit in us.

Although the end result is radical, the process is gradual, and while it is the work of the Spirit it is not something in which we are completely passive. Our part is to be submissive and being submissive isn't being passive. We should desire this work within us, yearn for its completion in our lives. In Philippians 3:10, when Paul says, 'that I may know Him and the power of His resurrection, and the fellowship of His suffering, being conformed to His death' he is expressing such a yearning.[2]

The kind of thought-life characteristic of the Philippians was having devastating consequences in their inter-personal and inter-church relationships. And because of the close link between thought and conduct it resulted in a distorted picture of Christ being presented before others, thus hindering evangelism as well. These problems and their consequences form the immediate context of Philippians 2:5-8, one of the greatest Christological passages in the Bible. It is in this context that Paul speaks these words:

> 'Let this mind be in you which was also in Christ Jesus, who, being in the form of God, did not consider it robbery to be equal with God, but made Himself of no reputation, taking the form of a servant, and coming in the likeness of men. And being found in appearance as a man, He humbled Himself and became obedient to the point of death, even the death of the cross...'

As an aid to the clarification of what is being taught here these two points must be considered: (i) v. 5, God's Command to all Christians (ii) vv. 6-8, Christ's Example for all Christians.

(i) v. 5 God's Command

It should be noted that verse 5 is a command. Although in our English text it may seem to be an option in the original, 'The present imperative (*phroneistho*)* shows that a humble, altruistic concern must be a daily practice and that it must originate within a submissive will which is determined to obey God.'[6] Perhaps the best translation of this phrase is, 'Have this mind in yourselves.'[7]

In its context, the command to have the mind of Christ looks back to the problems described in verses 2-4, and forward to their resolution through following Christ's example as outlined in verses 6-8. What is being said in verse 5 is critical to following this example. And where Paul begins in this verse is where we must all begin - with our minds. Dr. Francis Schaeffer has written that 'the internal thought world causes the external ... this is where true spirituality in the Christian life rests: in the realm of my thought life.'[8] To use Kepler's famous phrase, 'We must think God's thoughts after Him'.

Our minds are to reflect the mind of Jesus Christ. This, however, does not happen automatically when we accept Him as Saviour. As we have observed already it is a gradual and progressive experience. Some refer to this as progressive sanctification and, properly understood, it is a helpful term. Paul writes about this in many places in contrasting the old man with the new man in Christ. One example is found in Ephesians 4:17-24 where he develops this distinction, pointing to our past as characterized by darkened understanding, ignorance of God and spiritual matters, and alienation from the life God wants us to lead. In verse 17 he says we should 'no longer walk as the rest of the Gentiles walk, in the futility of their mind'. And in verses 20 and 23 he gives as the reason for this change in conduct the fact that we are to learn Christ and be 'renewed in the spirit of (our) mind'. Following on from this he concludes in verse 34 by listing righteousness and holiness as virtues which identify the new man.

The point is that the new man has a renewed way of thinking about everything which is reflected in his conduct. Having learned Christ, His example and its application, he is then different from the way he was before and from all others who have not so learned and applied Christ.

---

*Some Greek texts have *phroneite* (second person plural).

(ii) vv 6-8 Christ's Example

These few verses are not intended as an exhaustive statement by which the mind of Christ is to be defined. The characteristics related by Paul are those most directly pertaining to the problems facing the Philippian Christians. However, because these problems are so basic to us all, what is said serves as a general statement of its character and may be widely applied beyond the context.

We will consider in these verses seven important features of the mind and conduct of Christ. This passage, describing the 'humiliation of Christ', reveals His progressive condescension. It spans the greatest extremes, from the form of God to that of a servant, culminating in the greatest blessing to mankind, His substitutionary death on Calvary. As these seven features unfold one from another they disclose what is basic to the mind and conduct of our Lord.

(i) v 6 Christ was in the form of God:

In this verse the word form has nothing to do with external appearance, rather it is a statement about Christ's eternal nature. In verses 7 and 8 we are told that His *likeness* or *appearance* was that of man, that is what He looked like externally during His incarnation, but in *form* He was God. This is His true and abiding identity.

Kenneth Wuest writes that 'the Greek word for *form* refers to that outward expression which a person gives to His inmost nature. This expression is not assumed from the outside, but proceeds directly from within.'[9] Thus Christ's conduct, expressed in the verses which follow, arises from who He is intrinsically - God, and not who He appeared to be - man. This is an important distinction to be made, especially in light of its application in our lives.

The application involves who we really are. Following conversion our true and abiding identity is that of a 'new creation in Christ'. While in appearance we look like all others about us, our conduct is not determined by our external appearance, but by inward reality. Later in this same chapter Paul says, 'work out your own salvation with fear and trembling; for it is God who works in you both to will and to do for His good pleasure' (Phil 2:12,13). This does not imply working to attain salvation, but working because of salvation already received by God's grace. The meaning of working in this context may best be expressed by the word 'translate'. We are to translate who we are, which in eternal reality is a new creation in Christ, into the way we live. At the same time, we are being transformed by God in order that we may conform to the image of Christ. The remaining six steps will help us understand and accomplish this conformity.

(ii) v 6 He was equal with God

What Paul says here in full is that Christ 'did not consider it robbery to be equal with God'. This rather difficult phrase, when properly understood, reveals a powerful aspect of Christ's example. The wording in English is a bit puzzling but it becomes clearer as we consider another very acceptable translation. Christ 'did not consider the fact of being equal to God a prize to be selfishly grasped'[10]. The verb 'consider' refers to a past decision when Christ put aside His divine right to rule so that He could come to us and become our servant and Saviour. This is the same verb that Paul uses in verse 3 when he says 'let each esteem others better than himself.' Christ was not motivated by His rights nor by any desire for personal gain, but by the needs of others. For others, He laid aside this great glory and walked the path to the cross. If we are to follow in His footsteps we will be led to sacrificial service, for others.

(iii) v 7 He made Himself of no reputation

This expression is a translation of two Greek words whose literal meaning is that 'He emptied Himself'. This self-emptying is generally the idea developed in any study of this part of the verse. And the question naturally follows, 'Of what did He empty Himself?' The way we respond is very important. We know that He did not empty Himself of being God, that is an impossibility. Nor did He empty Himself of the use of His attributes as God. In the Gospels we read that from time to time He used these powers, as when He calmed the storm on the Sea of Galilee, healed the blind and cast out demons from those possessed. If He did not empty Himself in these ways, then what is the meaning of this phrase, and what is its application to us?

This question may be answered in two ways, both of which are part of the same answer.

First, Christ put aside the independent use of His attributes as God. All through His earthly existence He yielded completely to the will of His Father, using His powers as God always under the control of the Holy Spirit and in accordance with that will. His self-emptying is closely connected to the next step of His condescension, His taking the form of a servant. A servant, or more precisely as the Greek word here indicates, a bondslave, does not exercise his will independently but is submissive to his master. Such was the relationship assumed between the Son and the Father during the incarnation.

The second part of our answer is this. Jesus Christ emptied Himself of - self. He did not consider *self* of any importance. He considered Himself of no significance in light of the purpose of His life on earth. In a very beautiful way this fits into the overall teaching of this passage and clarifies what lies at the heart of many of our problems in life. It is easy for us to see how this applies to the Philippians. Instead of putting themselves first, they are to consider others, as Christ did. Of course this application is much broader than Philippi. It relates to believers of all time and in all places, to any who intend to follow the Lord.

This aspect of Christ's example is the thrust of His radical remarks in Matthew 16:24,25:

'If anyone desires to come after Me, let him deny himself, and take up his cross, and follow Me. For whoever desires to save his life will lose it, and whoever loses his life for My sake will find it.'

Christ in emptying Himself of self, obeyed perfectly and willingly the will of His Father and this is His example to us. We all do well to consider what part self plays in our lives as Christians. Of all the various aspects of Christ's example, this is certainly one of the most difficult to apply.

When the Apostle Paul wrote, "I have been crucified with Christ; *it is no longer* I who live, *but Christ* lives in me' the death of self is what he had in mind. This is what Hudson Taylor called *the exchanged life.*

(iv) v 7 He took the form of a servant

As we have already noted there is the closest connection between Christ's self-emptying and His taking the form of a servant/ bondslave. In a sense, Christ's emptying Himself of one thing - self, is accomplished by His taking up of another thing - His servant-form. So long as our own lives are full of self there will be little room for service to God or others. In assuming the form of a servant Christ declared several things. He made clear that He did not consider His life His own, it belonged to the Father. Also, by this act, He placed Himself under the authority of the Father - dramatically as a slave to a master. In doing this He assumed a position in which certain things were expected of Him and certain demands were made on Him.

Such an attitude as Christ expresses in this runs contrary to man's thinking. Throughout history men have striven to be their own masters and to control their own destinies, thinking that to do so is to be free. Again it is the radical teaching of Christ's example which breaks into our lives and compels us to consider Him. It is as we follow in His footsteps that we learn freedom is not the right to do what we want, but the strength to do what we should. Then we discover the truth of the words of George Matheson, 'Make me a captive Lord, and then I shall be free'.

(v) v 7 He came in the likeness of men

Christ's earthly appearance was as that of all other men. There was no halo. There was nothing supernatural about His physical form. We should remember that it was His conception, not His birth that was supernatural. His birth was just like ours. And the body into which He was born was similar in every way to our own.

The way people learned who He was was not because He *looked* different, but because He *was* different. His true identity as God was manifested in all His thoughts and actions. And, perhaps this was never more clearly seen than when He faced temptation. Like us, He was tempted in all areas, but unlike us, His temptation did not result in sin by yielding (Heb. 4:15).

It is relatively easy for us to rationalize about our own temptations and the consequent sin. Looking around us we can always find examples of those who have failed, and then justify our own failure. However, Jesus Christ, who, in true appearance was like men, was tempted but did not sin. There is an alternative affirmed by His example. While it may be natural to yield to temptation, the Christian is not natural, but supernatural, indwelt and empowered by the Spirit of God. Rather than doing what comes naturally, we are to do what comes supernaturally. Christ our Saviour and Example makes this possible. Our lives do not have to be ruled and ruined by sin. With this in mind we should consider carefully these words: 'Grace and peace be multiplied to you in the knowledge of God and of Jesus our Lord, as His divine power has given us all things that pertain to life and godliness, through the knowledge of Him who called us by glory and virtue, by which have been given to us exceedingly great and precious promises, that through these you may be partakers of the divine nature, having escaped the corruption that is in the world through lust' (2 Peter 1:2-4).

(vi) v 8 He humbled Himself

In considering this point it is important that we recognize what is being said - 'He humbled Himself'. No one humbled Him, it was His choice. What a mark of greatness this is. The whole of His incarnation, in all of its condescension, was an act of voluntary humiliation leading to the cross. Humility is a difficult quality to define and may best be communicated by description. And no description can excel that which is given to us in the life of Christ. The word humility means to be 'made low'. And the Lord of Life chose the lowest level, death and the grave. What becomes of all our pride in the shadow of such humility? Here is the 'lowliness of mind' Paul speaks of in verse 3 in its most perfect application.

There is a clear link between humility and obedience observed in Christ, 'He humbled Himself and became obedient'. All of His life reveals His obedience to the authority of God. His first recorded words are, 'I must be about My Father's business' (Luke 2:49). And among His final words before death were, 'It is finished' (John 19:30). What the Father had called Him to do was completed in humble obedience.

True humility is not self-abasement but living for God's glory. Humble obedience exalts the Father and is the pathway to our own exaltation. This is the pattern we find in Christ's life. Following His humiliation, Philippians 2:5-8, comes His exaltation, verses 9-11. His is the name above every name; all will bow before Him and acknowledge that He is Lord. Yet He came to this through the cross.

Christ's humility was not the means He chose to secure the end, that of exaltation. Such would have been a false humility. He simply placed Himself under the Father's hand, in obedience to His will. Because He did so He was exalted. By His example He says to us, 'humble yourselves under the mighty hand of God, that He may exalt you in due time' (I Pet. 5:6).

(vii) v 8, He was obedient to death, even crucifixion
The death on the cross for a Jew was a cursed way to die, for a Roman it was the death of a criminal, but for Christ Jesus it was the purpose of His incarnation. This is why He emptied Himself, became a servant and appeared as man. This is the reason behind His humility and obedience - death! Serving God the Father cost the Son everything. We should ask ourselves, 'What is it costing me to serve Him?'

Our spiritual life begins at the cross with the death of Christ. His death makes our life possible and our identification with Him makes it personal. In this spiritual sense there can be no life apart from death. Here we come again to Paul's words, 'I am crucified with Christ, nevertheless I live' (Gal 2:20). And to these we join another of his statements, 'I die daily' (1 Cor 15:31). The demand for dying to self does not end at the beginning of our spiritual life, it only begins there. In *True Spirituality* Francis Schaeffer has written,

'As Christ's rejection and death are the first steps in the order of redemption, so our rejection and death to things and self are the first steps in the order of true and growing spirituality. As there could be no next step in the order of Christ's redemption until the step of death was taken, so in the Christian there can be no further step until these first two steps are faced--not in theory only, but at least in some partial practice.'[11]

We are to practice death to self and things daily. Christ said, 'If anyone desires to come after Me, let him deny himself, and take up his cross daily, and follow Me' (Luke 9:23). It is in doing this that we place our feet in the prints He has left for us to follow.

References

1. Henry Bettenson, *Documents of the Christian Church* (New York: Oxford University Press, 2nd ed, 1963), pp. 68-73.

2. Thomas Torrence, *Space, Time & Incarnation* (Oxford: Oxford University Press, 1969), p. 52.

3. Frederick L. Godet, *The Gospel of John* (Grand Rapids: Zondervan Publishing House, 1970), p. 269.

4. John Hick, ed, *The Myth of God Incarnate* (London: SCM Press Ltd, 1977), p. 31.

5. C. S. Lewis, *Surprised by Joy* (New York: Harcourt, Brace & World, Inc, 1955), p.236.

6. Robert G. Gromacki, *Stand United in Joy* An Exposition of Philippians (Schaumburg, IL: Regular Baptist Press, 1980), p. 90.

7. J. Dwight Pentecost, *The Joy of Living* A Study of Philippians (Grand Rapids: Zondervan Publishing House, 1973), p. 66.

8. Francis A. Schaeffer, *True Spirituality* (Wheaton: Tyndale House Publishers, 1972), pp. 115,116.

9. Kenneth Wuest, *Wuest's Word Studies Philippians* (Grand Rapids: Wm. B. Eerdmans Publishing Company, 1942), p. 62.

10. Gromacki, p. 94

11. Schaeffer, op. cit., p. 26.

'In Him was life, and the life was the light of men. '

John 1:4

'What was He doing all that time From boyhood through to early prime, Was He then idle, or the less About His Father's business?'

Leslie Weatherhead, *His Life and Ours*

'When all is said and done the authentic records of his life and teachings are so brief that they could easily be printed in a single issue of one of our larger daily papers, and in these a substantial portion of the space, (would be) devoted to the last few days of his life.

Kenneth Scott Latourette, *A History Of Christianity*

'Christ came to save every age. Thus He came to us as an infant, a child, a youth, and a man. And in each one He lived as our example.'

Irenaeus

'And thus the red-cheeked country Boy stood unconfused and unafraid before the old teachers, astonishing them with His wisdom and His innocence; for a little child can teach great lessons to the wisest men.'

Robert Bird, *Jesus, The Carpenter Of Nazareth*

2

THE HIDDEN YEARS

Peter writes that grace and peace are multiplied to us through our knowledge of Christ (2 Peter 1:2). This knowledge is not simply an accumulation of facts, rather it is in the sense of *knowing* Christ personally through the Holy Spirit and the Word of God. It is knowing Him, not knowing about Him, that brings us peace and increased godliness. Yet knowing about Him, where He lived, the economic and social context of a first century Jewish carpenter's life helps us to know Him. Such knowledge is not an end in itself, but a means to our desired spiritual goal of a greater likeness to Christ.

Throughout history people have had a general interest in Christ's life and a special fascination for the 'hidden years'. This period covers the time between His return from Egypt to Nazareth till His departure from there as He began His public ministry. These years are the focus of this chapter, and, though little is told us about them it is important that we understand what God has revealed.

Although ours is an increasingly secular generation there are numerous indications of an interest in these years. One example comes from the New Age Movement which exerts a subtle and growing influence today. A prominent adherent to this movement is the actress Shirley MacLaine. Through her books many have become aware of New Age characteristics such as belief in a spiritual dimension beyond that perceived by our five senses. New Agers teach that we may enter into this dimension through the help of spirit guides who impart a greater understanding of the past, present and future. In Miss MacLaine's case she identifies one of her guides as Ramtha the Enlightened One. And in her book, *Dancing in the Light*, she writes that among the first things she asked Ramtha was for information about the personal life of Jesus Christ.[1]

In addition to New Age interest in the 'hidden years', the 1980's produced such books as *The Lost Years of Jesus*. This book bears an interesting sub-title which declares it to be 'Documentary evidence of Jesus' 17-year journey to the East'. In this intriguing work the author, Elizabeth Clare Prophet, says that because of a proposal of marriage, Jesus, not yet 14 years old, secretly left Joseph's house and began to journey east in search of perfection through personal devotion to God. His travels took Him through Pakistan, India, Ladakh, Nepal, Tibet, and back to Persia on His return to Palestine. Along the way He is said to have studied with those who had attained enlightenment. She writes that He became a disciple of the Brahmins in India with whom He studied the Vedas and then, in Nepal and Tibet, He examined the Buddhist scriptures under the guidance of Buddhist monks. In Persia He studied the documents of Zarathustra before returning to Palestine. There, at the age of 29, He began His public ministry of proclaiming the word of peace to the oppressed Jewish race.[2]

These references help confirm man's continuing curiosity about Jesus Christ - especially in those areas where God's Word is silent. Also, in nearly every life of Christ there are accounts of the fantastic claim made in apocryphal books such as *The Arabic Gospel of the Infancy* and *The Gospel of Thomas*. In them we read of Christ having shaped birds from river-bank clay and His delight when, upon clapping His hands, they came to life and flew away. We also read of Joseph, who was a poor craftsman and made inferior milk pails, gates and boxes, being helped by Christ who made them all perfect for him, even magically lengthening boards which he had cut too short.

Such stories as these combine to portray an extraordinary life lived by Christ during these years, and to present Him as someone with whom ordinary people like ourselves have nothing in common. This compulsion on man's part to fill in the gaps in Christ's life is caused in part by the lack of information given in Scripture.

Of the 89 chapters in the New Testament only 4 mention anything directly related to the 'hidden years'. In the first two chapters of both Matthew and Luke there are accounts of His birth and early life from the perspectives of the wise men and shepherds. These chapters tell of the star, angelic messages, Joseph's dreams and the journey to Egypt and back to Nazareth. Of the 4 only Luke chapter two contains anything about the nearly 30 years between His infancy and baptism.

In light of this comparative silence we should remember that the Bible tells us what we *need* to know and not always what we *want* to know. However, this observation serves to emphasize the importance of what we are told. We do need to know these things. The very nature of the Bible is revelation; God is revealing His truth to us, much of which we can know only because He tells us. All that He says is important. Yet, even when God speaks there are degrees of importance. It is man, not God, who refers to 'hidden years'. His revelation covers them in less detail, not because they are unimportant, but less important.

Why The Hidden Years?

Before we begin to study and apply the lessons found in the 'hidden years', let us ask a question which arises naturally from the way they are presented in Scripture. 'Why are we not told more about this part of Christ's life than we are?' In response there are several considerations. As I have said earlier, the Gospels are not a biography of Christ. Essentially they are preaching material, and as such they have a special purpose. That purpose is primarily to give us *the plan of salvation*. The most important thing for man is his eternal life and they tell us clearly and in detail how Christ provides for this. In a secondary sense they give us *a plan of living*. That is, they contain enough information about Christ's life to enable us to follow it as our pattern for life as believers.

The Gospels and Acts form the historical part of the New

Testament. The rest, with the exception of the Revelation, are doctrinal letters and much that is taught in them serves as amplification and application of the history given in the Gospels. Thus, in many cases, we are given the fact in its historical context as well as its practical application for our lives. Of course this still does not constitute a biography of Jesus Christ. God satisfies our needs, not our curiosity.

There is another reason for what we are told about this part of Christ's life. In his classic 19th century *Life of Christ*, F. W. Farrar suggests that 'We cannot imitate Him in the occupation of His ministry, nor can we remotely reproduce in our own experience the external circumstances of His life during those crowning years. But the vast majority of us are placed, by God's own appointment, amid those quiet duties of a commonplace and uneventful routine which are most closely analogous to the thirty years of His retirement; it was during these years that His life is for us the main example of how we ought to live'.[3]

In a more recent book, but along these same lines, Everett Harrison writes that 'the reason for the silence of Scripture is simply that there was nothing extraordinary to record ... It is Jesus' likeness to us, then, that shines through these narratives of the early years'.[4]

The lives of most of us are made up of ordinary events and experiences. And since the Christian life is a complete way of life, not one relating only to extremes of crisis or joy, what we learn about Christ in the home and workshop, as well as what Luke tells us in rel-ation to His visit to Jerusalem, touches our life at its most basic level.

When Jesus was baptized by John in the Jordan, the Father spoke from heaven and said, 'This is My beloved Son, in whom I am well pleased' (Matt. 3:17). The Father's announcement was His assessment of Jesus' quiet life in Nazareth. He pleased His Father then and if we follow His pattern we will please the Father now.

In his first letter Peter, writing about our redemption, says that it is secured 'with the precious blood of Christ, as of a lamb without blemish and without spot' (1 Pet. 1:19). Although his main point is the price paid for our salvation, he is also describing the purity of Christ's life. Paul uses similar terminology in writing about Christ's purpose for His church which is to 'present it to Himself a glorious church, not having spot or wrinkle or any such thing, but that it should be holy and without blemish' (Eph. 5:27). The church is composed of individual believers, each of whom are to please Christ by lives marked by purity and holiness, private and public.

In studying Christ's 'hidden years' we must focus on what we are told by God and not speculate about what we are not told. We begin with Nazareth where God incarnate spent more time than anywhere else.

Nazareth

The influence exerted upon the ancient and modern worlds by Palestine and its people has always been disproportionate to its size and population. The country measures about 150 miles in length, and the average width at its wider southern part is about 75 miles. When Christ lived there the population was not large and even today there are fewer than four million inhabitants.

The village of Nazareth where Jesus grew to manhood is in the northern Palestinian province of Galilee. Once part of David's kingdom, Galilee was lost to the Assyrians, regained during the Maccabeean era, and in Christ's day was ruled by Rome. Having been in the hands of Gentile leaders at various times it retained the strong imprint of their character in the first century as is evidenced by frequent references to it as 'Galilee of the Gentiles'.

In John 7:52 the Pharisees chided Nicodemus, saying, 'Search and look, for no prophet has arisen out of Galilee.' It was not a place from which any prophet had ever come, much less a place from which the Messiah might be expected. Often contrasted with Judea to the south, its people were considered boorish, lacking the distinctions of which Judea boasted as the home of orthodox teaching, the nation's shrines and institutions and the great Temple of Jerusalem itself.[5]

If Galilee and Nazareth were considered provincial by Judea it was not an entirely accurate assessment. Not only its past imparted a cosmopolitan quality, but its location added to it as well. Some spoke of it as being on the way to everywhere. A great road ran west from it to the Mediterranean Sea and east to the ends of the Roman Empire. From Damascus to the north a caravan route passed through it, heading for the bazaars of Egypt. The movement of armies, merchants and caravans along these roads made the province a window opening onto a wider world allowing its inhabitants, including the boy Jesus, to experience something of its exciting diversity and dimensions.

Galilee was where God planned that Jesus should grow up and He guided Joseph and Mary there through a dream (Matt. 2:22,23). And of all the villages in Galilee it was Nazareth to which Christ was brought and where He would remain until the time came for Him to begin His ministry to the Nation and the world.

It has been said of Christ that 'Circumstances did not make Him; God did'.[6] He was not the product of Palestine, Galilee or the mountain village of Nazareth. Nor, as Christians, are we the product of our environment. While it is true that it does have a measured impact on our lives, it is God who is the Potter and we the clay in His hands. It is He who moulds our lives. There is no source of spiritual life other than Him and any conformity to Him will be by His power also. Because of this truth Christianity transcends all time and place.

Nowhere in God's world is the best place to be, or to be from, neither village nor city, West or East. Nor do economic conditions, social level, or political context determine life for the Christian. Christ came from Nazareth of Galilee, from the simplicity of a carpenter's home to present Himself as the Saviour of men. He was the expected Messiah from a totally unexpected place. Because of this we learn that our service for God and growth in His likeness have nothing to do with geography or environment. The history of the church is filled with stories of those whom God has called and used from the most unlikely circumstances and obscure places.

Christ and the Family
In the Bible we learn that God has established three institutions for

the good of society: civil government, the church and the home. During His earthly life Christ lived in significant relationship with each of these three. He obeyed both civil and ecclesiastical law so long as doing so did not violate a higher law of God. And He laid the foundation for the church by His life and teaching, becoming Himself its 'Chief cornerstone' (I Peter 2:6-8). But it is as a family member that He most closely identifies with us during the 'hidden years'.

The house in which Jesus spent His early life was similar to that of most people living in first century Palestine. It was probably made from limestone quarried from the surrounding hills, or perhaps from sun-baked mud and straw. There would have been a single room to which, according to Eastern custom, the carpentry shop was attached. This would have been only a small room as much of the work was done outdoors. The floor of the house would have been covered by scattered rushes or woven mats. Along one wall a wooden seat was placed and a painted chest added a bit of colour and contained the family's possessions. In the room, scattered cushions, clay jars, their mouths stopped with herbs and spices to keep the contents fresh, and a wooden stool would have completed the furnishings. At meal time a tray was placed upon this stool and the family gathered about it to eat together. Light came from the open door and possibly a single oil lamp. The house would have stood along one of Nazareth's narrow, crooked streets and beyond it would be seen vineyards on terraced hillsides. The significant fact concerning Christ's Nazareth home is that it was typical of its place and time. Nothing Scripture tells us about His life suggests anything otherwise.

A house, even a humble one, does not make a home, it is the people living within it which does this. Jesus grew up as part of a large family by our standards. He was the eldest of at least seven children, four half-brothers and two half-sisters (Mark 6:3). They, along with Joseph and Mary, formed the family unit in which He was nurtured and grew.

It is impossible for us to evaluate the extent of His earthly parents influence upon Him in the home. The Bible by which

Joseph and Mary lived was the Old Testament and they would have understood well its Wisdom Literature, including Proverbs 22:6, 'Train up a child in the way he should go, And when he is old he will not depart from it.' In their Jewish context such training was not a casual thing. It was not something entrusted to others, not to the synagogue then, as it must not be left to the church today. Nor was it something done by only one of the parents. As the spiritual head of the home the greatest responsibility fell to the father, but it was not his alone. Proverbs 31:1, for example, indicates the mother's involvement as it refers to 'The words of King Lemuel, the utterances which his mother taught him'. Spiritual training was a shared responsibility, both parents being involved in teaching their family about God and His way of life.

It should be easy for us to see the importance of Christ's example of a godly and stable home life. No doubt there was divorce and remarriage in Nazareth. Infidelity, as well as all the other things which we name today as causes for the break up of the family structure existed then. But these things were not part of Christ's family life.

Among the first things God teaches us in the Bible is the sanctity of marriage, basing its oneness upon the unity existing between the members of the Trinity. What He says in Genesis 2:24 about this oneness is what Christ observed in His earthly parents. Perhaps no man has ever been so severely tested regarding marriage as Joseph was when he learned of Mary's virgin conception. Matthew 1:18 says that 'Mary was betrothed to Joseph', and the next verse confirms his commitment to their betrothal and marriage. From this point onwards Mary is called his wife in Scripture. Even this staggering situation did not destroy their relationship. How strongly this stands in opposition to our day when even slight things are considered sufficient reason for divorce.

The family context within which Christ lived was one where God's ideal was actualized: one man, one woman, joined till separated by death. This ideal is still His plan for us today. It is not His expectation nor our ability to fulfil it that has changed. It is our attitude toward marriage and family that has been altered, in part because of the subtle influence of secularisation. Secularisation means that basic beliefs and assumptions resting on the truth of the Bible are regarded as having little or no consequence for the conduct of life. As Christians we are not exempt from this influence and the decline of our conformity to Christ is paralleled by the increase of secularisation in society.

Simplicity

A carpenter's home in Jesus' day was one in which life was lived at a very basic level. Joseph and Mary gave Jesus security, love, understanding, an example of devotion to God, and along with these things the material needs of life, the latter being only a part of what good parents should provide. From Christ's teaching we learn something about what life in general was like then. In one of His parables He refers to a woman who, having lost a single coin, lit the lamp and swept the whole house to find it. When the disciples asked Him to teach them to pray, one of the requests He included in the Learner's Prayer He taught them was for their daily bread. It might have been His own home, in which there was daily dependence on God's supply, reflected in this prayer. As He grew up the loss of the smallest coin may have been critical to the family finances. If these are not His own experiences, they suggest the economic situation which prevailed and within which He lived and ministered.

Although Christ did not live in luxury, He was not an ascetic. During His public ministry He came eating and drinking and was criticized because His disciples did not fast as often as those of John or the Pharisees. He gives the essence of His teaching on simplicity of life and the place of material things in His Sermon on the Mount. In Matthew 6:33 He says, 'Seek first the kingdom of God and His righteousness, and all these things shall be added to you'.

Priority is the first emphasis of this statement. It is God first then material things. In Luke 16:13 He says, 'No servant can serve two masters: for either he will hate the one and love the other, or else he will be loyal to the one and despise the other. You cannot serve God and mammon.'

The order in which God or mammon appears in our lives identifies our master. Any move toward either one is a move away from the other. Few of us can conceive of the hold covetousness has upon us. In our age with its exaggerated belief in the importance of wealth and possessions the tension between the spiritual and the material is extreme.

Richard Foster has written that 'Jesus spoke to the question of economics more than any other social issue. If in a comparatively simple society our Lord would lay such strong emphasis upon the spiritual danger of wealth, how much more should we who live in a highly affluent culture take seriously the economic question'.[7] He says that 'Simplicity is the only thing that can sufficiently reorient our lives so that possessions can be genuinely enjoyed without destroying us. Without simplicity we will either capitulate to the *mammon* spirit of this present evil age, or we will fall into an un-Christian legalistic asceticism. Both lead to idolatry. Both are spiritually lethal'.[8]

Christ did not deny the value of the material and delight in poverty. But in the way He lived and by what He said He affirmed that God must rule our heart. It is possible to lead a holy life with a pocket full of money, but not with a heart full of it. He warns us, 'Do not lay up for yourselves treasures on earth ... but lay up ... treasures in heaven ... For where your treasure is, there your heart will be also' (Matt. 6:19-21). Sadly many today are like the rich young ruler of Christ's day who would rather own things than be owned by God.[9]

There are two aspects of simplicity taught by Christ's example. Of most importance is our heart attitude, to be expressed by placing God first. And second is a way of living which is its consequence. The material ought to be subordinate to the spiritual; that is, we own our possessions and ought not to be owned by them, nor by a desire to have more of them. This second characteristic can only come as it flows naturally from the first, and as it does it is evidence of conformity to Christ. Inward holiness is outwardly manifested, and in a materialistic age such as ours it will not go unnoticed.

Christ-like simplicity must begin in the heart. Any attempt to renounce outwardly material things while harbouring a covetous spirit within will destroy our peace and distort Christ's image before others. Hypocrisy too is a very observable characteristic.

Some are concerned, it seems, that to follow Christ in simplicity will mean the loss of all material things. But that is not what Christ taught, nor is it the way He lived. In Matthew 6:33 He does not speak against having possessions, rather He puts them in their proper place - after God's kingdom and righteousness. Simplicity does not demand life without possessions. But it does demand a spirit of renunciation which enables us to say 'no' to things. In the end 'It is willingness for simplicity that God wants us to have, though he may often allow us greater luxury than our bare needs demand'.[10]

Christ the Carpenter

In first century Jewish society, work was highly honoured. The Talmud declared it the duty of every father to see that his son learned a trade by which he could earn a living. And if he failed to do this it was considered the same as teaching him to be a thief.

The only occupation associated with Christ in His early life is that of a carpenter. This was the trade He learned from Joseph and probably practised at his side. Tradition says that Joseph died when Jesus was 13 years old. This is based on the lack of further reference to him following the visit to Jerusalem when Jesus was 12. If this was so it means that as the eldest son He became responsible for the needs of His family. Thus the work He did was motivated by necessity and love. Even if Joseph lived a few years longer, as the eldest Jesus would have shared in his work in a responsible way.

A great deal has been written about the meaning of the Greek word *tekton* which is usually translated 'carpenter'. This word does have a wider meaning and can refer to either a carpenter or a mason. There is also a relationship between it and our word 'technician', and in this sense it describes any skilled worker who 'brings forth', 'makes' or 'creates' an object.[11]

In the Near East, building involved working more with stone

and brick than with wood because of its scarcity. And as a *tekton* Christ probably possessed the skill required to build a house, a bridge or a wall. Also, because He worked in a small village, He would have spent some time mending household items such as chairs, tables and broken bread troughs.

Regarding Christ's work, the apologist Justin Martyr made an observation in the 2nd century which has often been quoted since then. He wrote that Christ 'was in the habit of working as a carpenter among men, making ploughs and yokes'.[12] Since then Christ has been associated especially with these implements, this being reinforced by His reference to them in teaching spiritual truths. In Luke 9:62 He warns us against putting our hand to the plough and looking back, suggesting that such inattention indicates our unfitness for God's kingdom.

Several times He mentions yokes in reference to the Christian life. In Nazareth two kinds were commonly made, one was for the purpose of uniting two oxen, enabling them to pull together in the field; the other was a wooden frame which was placed on a person's shoulders so that a load could more easily be carried by distributing its weight equally on both sides of the body. This is the one He refers to in Matthew 11:29,30 when He invites us to take up His yoke, saying, 'My yoke is easy and My burden is light.' The Greek word for 'easy' is *chrestos* which means that it is well fitting or properly adjusted so that it does not chafe the wearer. Concerning Christ's connection with such yokes there is a legend that says a sign hung above His carpentry shop which read, 'My Yokes Fit Well.' The implication being that they were the product of a good workman, one taking pride in what he did. Of course this is just a legend, but if it is not true, it's application is a valid one as the work Christ did would have been careful and skilled.

In all, Christ probably spent about 18 years working as a carpenter. I believe there are two keys to understanding the comparatively long time He spent in this way. The first is *timing*. In the Bible, at strategic places in his life, we find references to time:

(i) Galatians 4:4: 'But when the fullness of the time had come, God sent forth His Son, born of a woman, born under the law'.

Here the phrase 'fullness of time' simply means when the time was right. At that moment God sent Christ and He came willingly into our world.

(ii) John 2:4: In Cana of Galilee, when Mary spoke to Him about the lack of wine for the wedding which was the occasion of His first miracle, He replied, 'My hour has not yet come.'

(iii) John 7:6; 8:20: He told His unbelieving brothers and also the Pharisees at this later stage in His ministry that His 'hour had not yet come', referring to the time of His death.

(iv) John 17:1: A little more than three years after His words to Mary at Cana, He prays to His Father saying, '... the hour has come. Glorify Your Son, that Your Son also may glorify You ... I have glorified You on the earth. I have finished the work which You have given Me to do.'

Clearly the events of Christ's life were lived according to God's timing. During all His life He was 'about' His Father's business - even when He seemed to be only waiting and working in Nazareth.

Christ's life teaches us something about God's view of time. In the Psalms, Ethan laments, 'Remember how short my time is' (Ps. 89:47). And Paul reminds us in Ephesians 5:16 that we must 'redeem the time, because the days are evil'. We frequently refer to this verse as an inducement to action, but seldom follow it with the next which says, 'Therefore do not be unwise, but understand what the will of the Lord is' (Eph. 5:17). It is a characteristic of wisdom, after the pattern of Christ, to understand that time and God's will are inseparable. Too often we forget this and allow our choices and actions to be dictated by time rather than ruled by the will of God. And generally we interpret redeeming the time as being in a rush to get something done. I remember as a new theological student that my professor had these words inscribed on his study door, 'Make Haste Slowly'. This, he said, was the motto of theology. Perhaps it should be applied not just to theology, but to all of life. There is an old Filipino description of Westerners as 'people with gods on their wrists,'[13] a description that fits many Christians in our age of motion and hurry. Time is a harsh master and in serving it our allegiance to eternity may be forgotten.

Christ was on earth to transact business of an eternal nature and the pattern of His life shows us that 'To everything there is a season, A time for every purpose under heaven' (Eccl. 3:1). And under heaven His purpose was the carpenter's bench for what may seem to us a long time. But He was not wasting His time then any more than we are when we do our work as an extension of our true Christian selves, in God's name and for His glory. It is time wasted when our only concern is, 'How much will I be paid', rather than 'How should I do this work as a Christian?'

The second key to understanding Christ's time as a carpenter is *identification*. We spend a major part of our lives working at something and He identifies with us in this by doing the same, showing us the dignity of honest labour. To regard work in this way seems a novel idea today. Even as Christians, instead of viewing it as having dignity we may think of it as simply a result of the fall, the product of Adam's curse. We may simply accept it as a difficult task, often tedious, having to be endured - a necessity for survival.

However, part of the newness Christ brings to us is a restored attitude toward work. Everything He did was an extension of Himself, whether making yokes or doing miracles; His work declared who He was. While it may not be possible for us to change what our work is, it is possible for our attitude toward it to be changed and for us to bring our Christian principles to bear upon it. Not everyone reading this chapter will need to do this. Some already follow Christ here, but for many work is a separate compartment in their life, one of misery, not ministry, but we cannot separate our work from who we are as Christians. Christ did not categorize things in His life as secular and sacred, nor should we. All of our time belongs to God, all that we do should count for eternity. Christ viewed life as stewardship, a trust from God. We are poor stewards if all we do during our working lives is earn money.

Jesus, Jerusalem and the Temple
We come now to one of the most interesting sections in the Gospels concerning the life of Christ - Luke 2:40-52.

The 'hidden years' cover about ten times the length of His public ministry. And the single incident revealed in Scripture from them is contained in these 12 verses. Luke doesn't tell us much, but the brevity of what he says serves to heighten the importance of what took place when Jesus attended the Passover with His parents.

Jerusalem was not only the royal city of the Jewish Nation, it is the capital of the only kingdom God ever established on earth, and it will be the name of the future great city of His coming kingdom. Of all the cities in Palestine it is the one most closely associated with Christ. It was the setting of His death, burial, resurrection and ascension. It was to Jerusalem that He travelled at the age of 12 where He spoke His first words recorded in Scripture.

Jewish law required three annual visits to Jerusalem; at the times of Passover, Pentecost and the Feast of Tabernacles. In the process of time, those living outside of the city stopped coming to all three festivals, but nearly all who could do so made the journey to celebrate the Passover and remember God's deliverance of their ancestors from Egyptian captivity.

According to Luke, sometime during the days of Jesus' first Passover, Joseph and Mary decided to return to Nazareth. Jesus didn't go with them, although they assumed He was among those from their village who left together. Later, when they discovered His absence and returned to Jerusalem, they found Him at the Temple, listening to the teachers and asking them questions. When Mary expressed the concern she and Joseph had felt He said, 'Why is it that you sought Me? Did you not know that I must be about My Father's business?' (Luke 2:49) These are His first words found in the Bible and when they heard them they did not fully understand what He meant. Jesus, now reunited with His earthly parents, returned to Nazareth where He was 'subject to them ... and ... increased in wisdom and stature, and in favor with God and men' (Luke 2:51,52).

Thus we have Luke's record of this event in Christ's early life. We are told about it for a purpose. Certainly it marked a significant moment in His life. And there are several lessons we may apply from it to our own.

Growth

In both verses 40 and 52 Luke refers to Christ's growth. These verses stress His humanness, showing us that He was subject to the same laws of human development which apply in our own lives.

We have little difficulty thinking of Him growing physically; Isaiah 53:2 gives us an analogy which we readily accept: 'For He shall grow up before us as a tender plant, And as a root out of dry ground...' It seems quite natural to think of Him growing physically from an infant in Bethlehem to a man, full grown, striding out from Nazareth to begin His public ministry. Where we have difficulty is in thinking of Jesus Christ as God incarnate, yet growing in some way mentally and spiritually. But this is what Luke is saying. And for him to say anything less would be to diminish the degree of Christ's identification with us. It will help us understand how He could grow in these ways if we remember Paul's teaching in Philippians 2:7,8, of Christ's putting aside the independent use of His abilities as God for a time and taking the likeness and appearance of men.

He grew physically, mentally and spiritually; such balanced growth is normal. What is not normal is growth in only one or perhaps two of these areas, reaching physical maturity, experiencing a degree of mental development, but failing to grow spiritually. The reason this imbalance occurs in human growth is sin, but for the Christian that has been overcome in Christ and our development should proceed after His example.

It is an astonishing thing to think of Christ growing in some spiritual sense - what a degree of condescension and identification this implies. That He would do so is the strongest recommendation that we do so as well.

Regarding spiritual growth J. C. Ryle writes that 'to every one who is in downright earnest about his soul, and hungers and thirsts after spiritual life, the question ought to come home with searching power. Do we make progress in our religion? Do we grow?'[14] He says that our spiritual growth is 'an eminently practical subject, if any is in religion ... It is a leading mark of true saints that they grow'.[15]

Wisdom

Jesus sent His twelve apostles out commanding them to be 'wise as serpents and harmless as doves' (Matt. 10:16). He told them this because in the world to which they were going they would be as sheep among wolves. Wisdom would be needed for them to live and minister among the wolves of their day.

Again, in the first and last verses of this passage, Luke links Christ with an important virtue - wisdom. He says that He was 'filled with wisdom', and that He 'increased in wisdom'. Throughout His life His wisdom was recognized by men. No doubt this was what astonished the teachers at the Temple when He understood their lessons and asked them probing questions. Even then He possessed an insight into life and its purpose and meaning that amazed all who knew Him.

All wisdom is not the same. A study of the Scriptures reveals that there are two kinds. James defines these in his Epistle as follows.

(i) James 3:15: There is wisdom that 'does not descend from above, but is earthly, sensual, demonic'. This is what Paul calls the wisdom 'of this world', which is 'foolishness with God' (1 Cor. 3:19). It is wisdom which is earthly as opposed to heavenly, sensual as opposed to spiritual and demonic as opposed to Divine. John Bunyan characterizes it in the *Pilgrim's Progress,* by Mr. Worldly Wiseman whom Christian meets early in his pilgrimage. Rather than encouraging Christian on his way to the cross for deliverance, he advises him to turn aside to the village of Morality and be counselled by a gentleman named Legality. Worldly wisdom denies God, His way and His Word, it produces men who are wise in their own sight, but foolish in God's. And the way they choose may bring to them what passes for success before men, but which lasts only as long as life. Such earthly wisdom does not help us to live abundantly now nor does it prepare us for eternity.

(ii) James 3:17: But there is another kind of wisdom which is from above and is 'first pure, then peaceable, gentle, willing to yield, full of mercy and good fruits, without partiality and without hypocrisy'. The eight characteristics James uses to describe wisdom from above serve as a good description of Christ Jesus who is the personification of such wisdom. Paul calls Him 'the wisdom of God' (1 Cor. 1:24). And if we are to be heavenly-wise it can only be by becoming Christ-like.

If there was only one kind of wisdom it would be easier for us, we wouldn't have to choose. Because there are two we must choose between that of earth or heaven; one or the other will be brought to bear on all our choices and actions in life.

The wisdom of this world generally assumes the form of knowledge or information and has as its goal securing a living. While this is necessary, it isn't the best nor highest goal in life. Its rewards are immediate. It gains for us things and the temporary pleasure they bring. But it will not bring us to heaven, nor will it bring any of heaven to our souls in this life. This is earthly wisdom - it does not come from God. It does, however, form much of the context within which we live and its influence upon us is constant and insistent.

In 1982 John Naisbitt published a book titled *Megatrends* which quickly became a best-seller, the cover describes it as 'A Road Map To The 21st Century', and a 'Field Guide Of The Future'. Megatrends are, according to Naisbitt, ten new directions which are now in the process of transforming our lives. On the first page he says that none of these ten 'is more subtle, yes more explosive ... than the first, the megashift from an industrial to an information society'.[16]

Such a society is marked by a proliferation of information to such an extent that 'information pollution' is spoken of by some. There seems to be no end of new information in sight and some suggest that knowledge is doubling every year. The result of all this is a constantly changing pattern of life in which one can easily become overwhelmed by the sheer mass of new knowledge.

In his book, Naisbitt quotes David Birch of the Massachusetts' Institute of Technology, who says that 'We are working ourselves out of the manufacturing business and into the thinking business'.[17] Thus we are described as an information society, one in which the business at hand is thinking. This might be grasped as a redeeming feature were it not for the nature of the human mind and the object of its thoughts. The consensus of our age is non-Christian and secular. And the Christian mind is constantly subject to this subtle influence. Consequently, even among Christians most thinking concerns profit rather than the loss of our lives to Christ Jesus. Our thoughts are like wild creatures which must be brought 'into captivity to the obedience of Christ' (2 Cor. 10:5). If they are not centred in Him and leading us to conformity with Him, they are leading us contrary to Him. Thinking, like faith, is no better than its object!

Jesus is 'the wisdom of God' (1 Cor. 1:24). In Him 'are hidden all the treasures of wisdom and knowledge' (Col. 2:3). We are wise when we want to be like Him. In the introduction I said that God wants us to be holy. He wants us to respond in all life's situations as He would and He shows us how to do this through the incarnation. He also wants us to be wise, to see everything in life from His point of view. Again He shows us how through the incarnation.

In *The Rock* ,T. S. Eliot asks these questions, 'Where is the wisdom we have lost in knowledge? Where is the knowledge we have lost in information?'[18] The only answer is - in Jesus Christ. He grew in wisdom while on earth and we must follow Him in this, growing wise in His truth, for we too must live and minister among wolves.

Priority

First and final words spoken are always important, and more so when they are Christ's. He spoke seven times from the cross at the end of His life. The sixth of His seven sayings was, 'It is finished' (John 19:30). These three words sum up His 33 years on earth and bring to a conclusion the declaration He makes in His first recorded words. In the Temple, in reply to Mary, He said, 'Why is it that you sought Me? Did you not know that I must be about My Father's business?' His Father's business was the business of all His life. He possessed singleness of mind and purpose which enabled Him always to do God's will and to always please Him. His first words teach us two things about the priorities in His life.

First they express His *priority in relationships*. In verse 48 Mary said, "Your father and I have sought You anxiously." She referred to Joseph, His earthly father. In His reply He distinguishes between Joseph and God, His Heavenly Father. Speaking of His Heavenly Father is not a denial of His true earthly relationship with Joseph. But in doing so He establishes a clear contrast: God and man, heavenly and earthly relationships. And here, in His first words, He teaches us where our allegiance must lie - where His did, with God.

In Matthew 10:37 Christ makes a startling statement when He says, "He who loves father or mother more than Me is not worthy of Me. And he who loves son or daughter more than Me is not worthy of Me." In verse 34 He states that He did not come to earth 'to bring peace but a sword'. Although He is the Prince of Peace and shares this peace with us, faith in Him is often the cause of some of the sharpest divisions on earth. Christ is constantly demanding that we make choices: God or mammon, earthly or heavenly wisdom, even choosing between a parent or child and Himself. In Colossians 1:18 Paul writes that in everything relating to His Church Christ should have the 'pre-eminence'. Pre-eminence is from the Greek work *protos,* meaning that in all things Christ must be 'first'. He is to stand before everyone else with whom we have a relationship. 'To belong to Christ is a privilege so inestimable that no other relationship can replace it. It is a duty so imperative that no other obligation is more binding.'[19]

There is no doubt that as Jesus spoke to Joseph and Mary that day in Jerusalem, He loved them. But He loved God more and regarded Him as pre-eminent in His life. Placing Christ first in our lives will not exclude others. It will actually enable us to have a relationship with them which is based, not upon selfish love, but Christ-like love. The word 'love' has lost nearly all of its true meaning in our sad world. It is a concept with little content, and it will remain as such until people acknowledge Christ as Lord, and submit to His rule in their relationships.

The second thing we learn from Christ's first words is His

priority in responsibilities: 'I must be about My Father's business.'

More than 20 years later Jesus would make His final visit to Jerusalem, again at the time of the Passover. Then He would predict His death on the cross, saying, "Now My soul is troubled, and what shall I say? Father, save Me from this hour? But for this purpose I came to this hour" (John 12:27). We cannot think of Christ apart from His cross. It was in the shadow of Calvary that He passed all His days on earth. The cross was the responsibility the Father laid on the Son from before the foundation of the world. And when they laid its wooden form upon His shoulder, compelling Him to carry it to the place of His death, He was living the hour for which He had come to earth, fulfilling and finalizing His Father's business.

The cross was not all of the Father's business for Christ. Remember, He said these words when He was 12 years old. He then went back to Nazareth with Joseph and Mary and presumably took up the trade of a carpenter. At the age of 30 He put aside His tools and left home to begin His life as a public figure - the promised Messiah.

His public ministry began at His baptism and one of the notable features of this transitional event was the voice of the Father heard from heaven, saying, 'This is My beloved Son, in whom I am well pleased' (Matt. 3:17). This announcement made it clear that He was pleased with the life of the Son throughout the 'hidden years'. He had been doing the Father's business in the years before He came to the Jordan as He had in His three years public ministry before He came to Calvary. This is an important observation, important because He spent years doing what we spend years doing, and all the while He was pleasing the Father, engaged in His work. All too often we fall prey to the dualism which has plagued Christianity for centuries creating in our thinking and conduct the divisions of sacred and secular.

During my early years as a Christian, where I lived, it was common to make a sharp distinction between those who were entering 'full time Christian service', and those who were not. While this distinction serves to place a greater responsibility upon those serving as pastors and missionaries, it also lessens the sense of responsibility for those who are not. Christ's example is not just for some, but for all Christians. His priority in responsibilities applies to each one of us.

Obedience

Luke 2:51 tells us that when Christ left the Temple in Jerusalem He went home to Nazareth with Joseph and Mary and was 'subject to them'. This means simply that He obeyed them. In Jerusalem He had declared His deity and equality with God. And as God He might have assumed His rightful position of authority over His earthly parents, but He did not. Obedience characterized His life throughout, He obeyed His Father in heaven and His parents on earth.

Harry Blamires writes that 'Because Christianity is a religion of revelation, of God's will made known in history, it follows that the moral keynote of Christianity must be obedience'.[20] God's revelation takes the form of His written Word, the Bible, and the Living Word, Christ. Both in word and deed He discloses His will for us. There is no justification for a plea on our part that we do not know what He expects from us. What He has every right to expect is obedience to what He has commanded in the Bible. But obedience is not a popular concept in a society characterized by the casting off of moral restraint. Blamires suggests that such a desire for liberation has taken many forms in our secular world. 'Labour is being 'freed' from the slavery of capitalists, women from servitude to men, children from the tyranny of pedagogues, students from rigid academic disciplines, citizens from the constraints of poverty, women from the tyranny of ovulation, homosexuals from laws against perversion, couples from the prison of lifelong marriages, pregnant women from consequent labour.'[21]

It seems that we hear someone calling for freedom from just about everything. Yet our example, Jesus Christ, obeyed God, parents, civil and ecclesiastical law. He always obeyed God and He obeyed all other forms of authority established by Him so long as it did not involve a violation of God's law.[22]

Christ's obedience is characterized by two distinctives. The first, *the extent of His obedience*, is stated in Philippians 2:8, 'He humbled Himself and became obedient to the point of death, even the death of the cross'. He obeyed even when to do so meant the greatest personal sacrifice possible. His was not obedience only when convenient or undemanding. Nor was He *selective in His obedience*, which is the second distinctive. He did not obey some of God's commands and ignore the rest. One area in which we are often faced with selective obedience is in the temptation to obey the letter but not the spirit of the law. In the Sermon on the Mount Christ teaches us that if we do not commit the acts of adultery or murder, but lust after a woman in our heart or hate our brother without a cause, we have not obeyed God. The first we find far easier than the second and we deceive ourselves if we think we have obeyed God's law when it is only the letter to which we have conformed. Such was not Christ's example and the demand for the inner obedience of our heart comes directly from His teaching and life.

The night before His crucifixion Christ spoke to His disciples about obedience: 'He who has My commandments and keeps them, it is he who loves Me. And he who loves Me will be loved by My Father, and I will love him and manifest Myself to him' (John 14:21). He made obedience the test of their love for Him. Similarly, it is obedience to His commandments that demonstrates our love for Him and, as a consequence, shows His reality and love. For in obeying them our lives are conformed to His, revealing Him through us to others.

Christ did not restrict the extent of His obedience nor was His obedience selective. On earth His life was not His own, but God's. And our life on earth is not our own, but His. Calvin Miller writes in *The Table of Inwardness* that 'The single most important word in the New Testament is Lord ... The issue of every disciple is whether or not he or she shall have a lord or be one'.[23] Our Lord is the one whom we obey.

I believe some of the most important words about Christ's life during the 'hidden years' are those we have already referred to and which will form an important part of the next chapter. They are words spoken by the 'voice' from heaven at the transition from Christ's private to public ministry. 'This is My beloved Son, in whom I am well pleased' (Matt. 3:17).

Christ was on the cross six hours, then He said, 'It is finished,' and it was, for then He died (John 19:30). He was on the earth 33 years before coming to Calvary. There could have been no brief ending had there not been the long 33-year beginning! More saw Him live than witnessed His death.

What pleased the Father about the Son? Was it the final six hours? the last three years or so before the cross? the quiet slow-flowing 30 years of life in Nazareth? It was all of these of course. Jesus said, 'I always do those things that please Him' (John 8:29). To follow in His footsteps is to do the same. At home, at work, in our finances, possessions, relationships, priorities, in all our choices we are to be like Him.

Where most of us are now living in our Christian lives is in Nazareth. We are caught up in our own 'hidden years' which, as we have observed, are not hidden at all. God sees, and that is what matters most. But our own world is also watching and the image they see of Christ is the one represented in us.

> You are our epistle written in our hearts, known and read by all men: you are manifestly an epistle of Christ, ministered by us, written not with ink but by the Spirit of the living God, not on tablets of stone, but on tablets of flesh, that is, of the heart (2 Cor. 3:2,3).

References

1. Shirley MacLaine, *Dancing In The Light* (New York: Bantam Books, 1985), p. 120.
2. Elizabeth Clare Prophet, *The Lost Years Of Jesus* (Livingston, Montana: Summit University Press, 1984), pp. 258-261.
3. Frederick W. Farrar, *The Life Of Christ* (London: Cassell Peter & Galpin, n.d.), p.72.
4. Everett F. Harrison, *A Short Life Of Christ* (Grand Rapids, Michigan: Eerdmans Publishing Company, 1979), pp. 63,64.
5. George Adam Smith, *The Historical Geography Of The Holy Land* (London: Hodder & Stoughton, 1900), p. 16.
6. A. M. Fairbairn, *Studies In The Life Of Christ* (London: Hodder & Stoughton, 1898), p. 46.
7. Richard Foster, *Celebration Of Discipline* (London: Hodder & Stoughton, 1980), pp. 73,74.
8. *Ibid*. p. 74.
9. Calvin Miller, *The Table of Inwardness* (Basingstoke, England: Marshall Pickering, 1984), p. 44.
10. Howard Guinness, *Sacrifice* (Downers Grove, Illinois: InterVarsity Press, 1975), p. 14.
11. William Hendriksen, *Exposition of the Gospel According to Mark* (Grand Rapids, Michigan: Baker Book House, 1981), p. 222.
12. *Ibid*..
13. Os Guinness, *The Gravedigger File* (London: Hodder & Stoughton, 1983), p. 40.
14. J. C. Ryle, *Holiness* (Welwyn, England: Evangelical Press, 1976), p. 83.
15. *Ibid*. p. 85.
16. John Naisbitt, *Megatrends* (New York: Warner Books, Inc., 1982), p. 1.
17. *Ibid*. p. 8.
18. T. S. Eliot, *Selected Poems* (London: Faber & Faber, 1954), p. 107.
19. William Hendriksen, *The Gospel of Matthew* (Edinburgh: The Banner of Truth Trust, 1974), p. 476.
20. Harry Blamires, *Meat Not Milk* (Lottbridge Drove, England: Kingsway Publications, 1988), p. 109.
21. *Ibid*. p. 110.
22. Francis A. Schaeffer discusses the Christian's responsibility to the state in chapters 7-9 of *A Christian Manifesto* (Westchester, Illinois: Crossway Books, 1981.), pp. 89-130.
23. Miller, *op cit*, p. 79.

Then Jesus came from Galilee to John at the Jordan to be baptized by him.

Matthew 3:13

Baptism signifies that the old Adam in us is to be drowned by daily sorrow and repentance, and perish with all sins and evil lusts; and that the new man should daily come forth again and rise, who shall live before God in righteousness and purity for ever.

Martin Luther, *Sermons*

It is the crossing of the Rubicon. If Caesar crosses the Rubicon, there will never be peace between him and the Senate again. He draws his sword, and he throws away the scabbard. Such is the act of baptism to the believer. It is the burning of the boats; it is as much to say, 'I cannot come back again to you, I am absolutely buried to you; I have nothing more to do with the world; I am Christ's and Christ's forever'.

Charles Spurgeon, *Sermons*

Therefore we were buried with Him through baptism into death, that just as Christ was raised from the dead by the glory of the Father, even so we also should walk in newness of life.

Romans 6:4

3

THE BAPTISM OF CHRIST

Mark introduces the next phase of the life of Christ by saying, 'It came to pass in those days that Jesus came from Nazareth of Galilee, and was baptized by John in the Jordan' (Mark 1:9). Until that time the scene of His life had been Nazareth for nearly thirty years, now it would be the Nation and the world. And the point of transition from one to the other was Bethabara, a ford of the Jordan about thirteen miles south of where it flowed out of the Sea of Galilee. The event marking this transition was Christ's water baptism at the hands of His cousin John.

Each of the four Gospels contains an account of Christ's baptism but it is Matthew's which provides the most detail. Thus it is his account – Matt. 3:13-17 – which will be the focus of our study in this chapter.

Before we begin to examine these verses a word must be said about baptism in general and the presuppositions underlying our approach to it. Views on baptism in general vary as not everyone thinks of it in the same way. When I speak of baptism there are two basic presuppositions which form the basis of my remarks. The first of these is that by water baptism I mean believer's baptism. That is, baptism following salvation. This is not necessarily adult baptism, as some might describe it - for children, even at quite a young age, can be saved. Their's is the child-like faith we must all have if we are to come in repentance to Christ for new life.

My second presupposition is that baptism is by immersion. This mode gives the clearest picture of what is symbolized by this ordinance - Christ's death, burial and resurrection and our identification with Him in these areas. While it is not the object of this chapter to attempt to prove these two things, they are important and are inherent in what will be said.

Baptism did not originate with John the Baptist but is a practice older than Christianity itself. It was a part of the rites of some ancient mystery religions and may have been, as some suggest, a spiritualization of the Levitical washings practised in Judaism before the time of Christ.[1] Until John emerged from the Judean wilderness and began to announce the coming Messiah offering water baptism as a sign of repentance it had been primarily associated with purification and cleansing. As Charles Ryrie points out it was generally a self-imposed rite in the context of Judaism, an act performed in sight of the rabbis by a proselyte.[2] But with John's coming it gained an altogether new significance because he associated it with repentance from personal sin and a thorough transformation from the old to a new life. His powerful exhortation was to 'flee from the wrath to come ... and bear fruits worthy of repentance' (Matt. 3:7,8). This was the prerequisite for the baptism he administered and only those who demonstrated a changed life were baptized by him.

In considering the biblical doctrine of baptism there are two extremes to be avoided. The first is that of making it the means of salvation - baptismal regeneration, or regarding it as a means of securing grace in a sacramental sense. The second is to either disregard it completely or to attach only an indifferent significance to it. Most heresies arise from pushing a truth to an extreme and this applies to water baptism as well. It is neither a means of grace nor a doctrine we may disregard. It is important. It is something Christ did and we are to follow Him, receiving it as an act of obedience to both His example and command (Matt. 3:13-17; 28:19,20).

Why Was Christ Baptised?
The baptism administered by John was 'unto repentance' (Matt.

3:11). As such it was universal in its application because from Adam to ourselves all have sinned and need to repent. This is the issue which introduces the problem relating to Christ's baptism by John. He is the only one ever to live on earth entirely free from personal sin. His contact with sin was because He acted as our substitute. While He would atone for our sin, there was no need for Him to repent of it.

The distinction between Christ and all others, including even the godly John, was made clear when He came to him for baptism. John hesitated, he said, "I have need to be baptized by You, and are You coming to me?" (Matt. 3:14). To this Jesus replied, "Permit it to be so now" (Matt. 3:15). Notice the difference. John said that he *needed* to be baptized, Jesus said, *permit* Me to be baptized. God's plan included making 'Him who knew no sin to be sin for us, that we might become the righteousness of God' (2 Cor. 5:21), by becoming 'The Lamb slain from the foundation of the world' (Rev. 13:8), who in the course of time became 'The Lamb of God who takes away the sin of the world' (John 1:29), by making 'His soul an offering for sin' (Isa. 53:10). He did all of this for us but He had no sin of His own. Therefore there was no need for Him to experience John's baptism for repentance. Nevertheless He requested it for reasons having nothing to do with His sin, but everything to do with ours.

Why was Christ baptized? The best way to respond to this question is to allow Him to speak for Himself. His first recorded words were spoken to Mary at the Temple in Jerusalem. He said, 'I must be about My Father's business' (Luke 2:49). His next recorded words form His reply to the question before us. In Matthew 3:15 He says, 'Permit it to be so now, for thus it is fitting for us to fulfil all righteousness.' This was part of His work on earth, but just what does it mean for Him to 'fulfil all righteousness'?

To understand this, we must first of all know something of what the Bible says about 'righteousness'. Perhaps Paul is the one most suited to clarify this doctrine as in Romans alone he refers to it at least 60 times in various ways. An evaluation of his comments from this book form a composite statement defining righteousness. Here is what he says (Romans 1:16,17): 'For I am not ashamed of the gospel of Christ, for it is the power of God to salvation for everyone who believes, for the Jew first and also for the Greek. For in it the righteousness of God is revealed from faith to faith; as it is written, "The just shall live by faith." '

This 'righteousness', the key to understanding Romans, Paul teaches us is revealed in the Gospel of Christ - His death and resurrection. It is revealed in His death because by it God punishes sin; revealed in His resurrection because by it God makes salvation possible for all who believe.[3] That faith in the finished work of Christ is the way by which we become righteous is clarified by Paul in Romans 3:21,22: 'But now the righteousness of God apart from the law is revealed, being witnessed by the Law and the Prophets, even the righteousness of God which is through faith in Jesus Christ to all and on all who believe.'

In relation to this Christ said of Himself that He had not come to destroy but to fulfil the Law and the Prophets (Matt. 5:17), and His first formal step on the pathway taking Him into His public ministry and on to the cross and empty tomb was this step into the Jordan to be baptized by John. Upon completion of His journey from Bethabara to Golgotha He fulfilled the Law, the Prophets and the righteousness of God, thus establishing the foundation for our faith.

Now let us consider Christ's baptism as it relates to our own. In order to do this we will examine two words which provide added clarification to the relationship between the two.

Identification

It bears repeating that incarnation is identification. In His baptism Christ identifies intimately with all of our lost race, with all who require baptism representing repentance for sins.

F. F. Bruce points out that 'Unlike those others who were baptized by John in the Jordan, confessing their sins, it was with no consciousness of sin that He accepted baptism, but with the resolution to place Himself unreservedly at God's disposal for the accomplishment of His saving purpose--and if, in doing so, He associated Himself publicly with sinners, that was something which He was going to do throughout His ministry, until He was "numbered with the transgressors" on the cross'.[4]

It is this which is behind what the writer of Hebrews means when he says, 'For both He who sanctifies and those who are being sanctified are all of one, for which reason He is not ashamed to call them brethren ... Inasmuch then as the children have partaken of flesh and blood, He Himself likewise shared in the same, that through death He might destroy him who had the power of death, that is, the devil ...' (Heb. 2:11,14). Christ was our Representative and our Substitute, becoming through His death and resurrection, our Redeemer.

Of course identification works two ways. As He identified with us in His life on earth there flows from this His command that we identify with Him in our life on earth! And an important part of this identification leads us to baptism. Baptism, His and ours, is a mutual affirmation of our solidarity with one another. On our part it declares openly that we have received Him as Saviour and Lord of our life, demonstrates our obedience to His example and command, and while it does not impart grace to save us, it does open our lives to greater grace which comes only as we follow and obey Him.

Illustration

The second word I want to suggest as an aid to understanding Christ's baptism is - illustration. By His baptism Jesus presented a vivid picture of what soon lay ahead as He fulfilled the righteous demands of the Father. Placed at the heart of this was His obedience. We have already observed that His obedience was not partial nor selective. As Paul points out in Philippians 2:6-8, Christ's identification with us as man and servant leads to His obedience 'to the point of death, even the death of the cross'. In His obedience is bound up our salvation and sanctification, the beginning and continuing of our identification with Him. Hebrews 10:9,10 says, 'He said, "Behold I have come to do Your will, O God" ... By that will we have been sanctified through the offering of the body of Jesus Christ once for all'. Our salvation and sanctification are based upon His obedience.

Matthew tells of an encounter Christ had with a group of elders and priests in the temple. They questioned His authority and He turned the tables on them with a question, 'The baptism of John, where was it from? From heaven or from man?' (Matt. 21:25) He caught them in 'catch 22 '- if they said 'man' the multitude who regarded John as a prophet, and whom they feared, would riot. If they said 'heaven' they knew He would say, 'Why then did you not believe him?' So they pleaded ignorance, indirectly affirming that it was from heaven - ordained of God. Thus Christ identified the origin of John's baptism. As believers we must all stand where the elders and priests stood - before Christ, facing this same question. We must choose, is baptism from man or God? Yet, if we are obedient the choice has been made for us. Christ, our Example, obeyed, receiving baptism, as He always obeyed the demands of Heaven.

Baptisms formed the brackets of Christ's public ministry, laying one each at its beginning and its ending. The second baptism in Christ's life, similar to His first, illustrates another aspect of our baptism. When He spoke of the end of His earthly life, of His suffering and death, He referred to it as a baptism (Matt. 20:22; Luke 12:50). What He experienced at John's hands, as he laid Him beneath the waters of the Jordan, foreshadowed what He would experience at God's hands, as He placed Him beneath the figurative waters of death, in the tomb. The picture is then made complete as He came up out of the River Jordan as He would later come forth from the Garden grave, alive and with power. In His public ministry He moved from baptism of water to baptism of death and in the distance between the two He fulfilled God's righteousness so that 'we might become the righteousness of God in Him' (2 Cor. 5:21).

Both identification and illustration relate to our baptism. In Romans 6:3,4, Paul says, 'Do you not know that as many of you as were baptized into Christ Jesus were baptized into His death?

Therefore we were buried with Him through baptism into death, that just as Christ was raised from the dead by the glory of the Father, even so we also should walk in newness of life.'

The New Testament speaks of two baptisms for the believer: water baptism and baptism of the Holy Spirit. Holy Spirit baptism will be considered shortly, however, both it and water baptism are pictured by Paul's words. Our water baptism illustrates our identification with Christ in His death, burial and resurrection to new life. Through water baptism I place myself publicly on the pathway He followed and announce that 'I have been crucified with Christ, it is no longer I who live, but Christ lives in me; and the life which I now live in the flesh I live by faith in the Son of God, who loved me and gave Himself for me' (Gal. 2:20). Our water baptism is important. It illustrates our new life, it is an act of obedience to Christ's example and command. By it is affirmed our baptism in the Holy Spirit; it is the external counterpart of that internal experience.

The Phenomena Which Followed Christ's Baptism

Immediately after Christ was baptized three notable things happened: the heavens were opened to Him, the Holy Spirit came down upon Him and a 'voice' spoke from heaven to Him. This voice we know to have been that of God because of what was said, and it, along with the presence of the Spirit upon the Son, marks one of the most significant representations of the Trinity to be found in Scripture. All of heaven was involved in this initial step of Christ on His public ascent to the Cross. Each member of the Trinity had an important part to play in the redemption secured. Let us consider these three remarkable phenomena one by one.

(i) The heavens were opened to Him

This is Matthew's account of what happened first. It is just like the other Gospel accounts with the exception of an interesting inclusion by Luke which says that Christ was praying when this took place (Luke 3:21). Here, as with many references to His prayers, we do not know what He said. I mention the following only as a matter of interest, and because it does seem to fit the occasion.

Alfred Edersheim suggests in *The Life and Times of Jesus The Messiah* that the prayer Christ offered then was the one He later taught the disciples, what we call 'The Learner's' or 'Lord's Prayer'. Of nearly 50 sources considered, Edersheim is the only one to make any suggestion concerning the content of this prayer. However, since he often has unusual insight into things overlooked by other writers, it is worth taking what he says into account. Here is what he writes about the prayer in relation to Christ's prayer at His baptism:

'We might individualize and emphasis in their application its opening sentences: "Our Father Which art in heaven, hallowed be Thy Name! Thy Kingdom come! Thy will be done in earth, as it is in heaven!" The first thought and the first petition had been the conscious outcome of the Temple-visit, ripened during the long years at Nazareth. The others were now the full expression of His submission to Baptism. He knew His Mission; He had consecrated Himself to it in His Baptism: "Father Which art in heaven, hallowed by Thy Name". The unlimited petition for the doing of God's will on earth with the same absoluteness as in heaven, was His self-consecration: the prayer of His Baptism, as the other was its confession. And the "hallowed be Thy Name" was the eulogy, because the ripened and experimental principle of His life. How this Will, connected with "the Kingdom", was to be done by Him, and when, He was to learn after His baptism.'[5]

Although we do not know what He prayed, we know that He did so. And because He did 'The heavens were opened to Him'. Such a striking connection surely contains a lesson for us in our Christian walk. Jesus was in the place of obedience - the waters of baptism, when He prayed and heaven opened and all Heaven responded! What a dramatic picture of prayer that produces results. Obedience to God provides access to God.

In relation to this it is interesting that in Mark's account of Christ's baptism he uses the root Greek word *schizo* referring to the heavens parting. The only other time he uses this word is in 15:38

where he relates it to the veil of the temple which was 'torn in two from top to bottom' at the death of Christ.⁶ The 'rending' of both the heavens and the veil provides access to the Father. In every way Christ is the Way-maker, the 'way, the truth, and the life', the only access we have to God (John 14:6). And it is through obedience that He secures for us this way, opening it to all who will obey and come to Him by faith. Therefore, obedience is a distinctive mark of our discipleship for discipleship is follow-ship.

(ii) And He saw the Spirit of God descending like a dove and alighting upon Him.

There are two great descents of the Holy Spirit in the New Testament. The first is here as He comes upon Christ at His baptism. The second is His coming upon Christ's followers after His resurrection and ascension to heaven. In each of these His coming represents an enduement of power.

To understand what the descent of the Spirit means at Christ's baptism we must know something about what Scripture teaches concerning Christ in relation to the Holy Spirit. The Old Testament clearly implies that Christ was filled with the Spirit from His conception. Isaiah especially speaks of Him in relation to the Spirit in such passages as Isaiah 11:1,2: 'There shall come forth a Rod from the stem of Jesse, and a Branch shall grow out of his roots. The Spirit of the Lord shall rest upon Him, the Spirit of wisdom and understanding, the Spirit of counsel and might, the Spirit of knowledge and of the fear of the Lord.' And again in Isaiah 42:1: 'Behold! My Servant whom I uphold, My Elect One in whom My soul delights! I have put My Spirit upon Him; He will bring forth justice to the Gentiles.'

That Christ was filled with the Spirit from conception is also implied from what Luke says about John the Baptist: 'For he will be great in the sight of the Lord, and shall drink neither wine nor strong drink. He will also be filled with the Holy Spirit even from his mother's womb' (Luke 1:15). If the same were not true of Jesus, John would then have been superior to Him because of this filling. John certainly did not think of himself in this way, he said: 'He who is coming after me is mightier than I, whose sandals I am not worthy to carry. He will baptize you with the Holy Spirit and fire' (Matt. 3:11). The biblical consensus is that Christ possessed the fullness of the Holy Spirit throughout His life.[7]

The New Testament shows Him in a special relationship with the Spirit:

(i) Matthew 1:20: He was born of the Holy Spirit;
(ii) Matthew 3:16; John 3:34: He was filled with the Holy Spirit without measure;
(iii) Luke 4:1,2: He was led by the Holy Spirit;
(iv) Luke 10:21: He rejoiced in the Holy Spirit.

The relationship existing between the Son and the Spirit is one which may also be experienced by those for whom the Son is Saviour:

(i) John 3:7,8; Titus 3:5: Our new birth is by the power of the Holy Spirit;
(ii) Ephesians 5:18: we are to be filled with the Holy Spirit;
(iii) Romans 8:14; Galatians 5:18: we are to be led by the Holy Spirit;
(iv) Philippians 3:3: we are to rejoice in Christ as He rejoices in the Holy Spirit.

Perhaps a point of clarification will be helpful at this juncture as we consider the baptism of the Holy Spirit. In the New Testament a distinction is made between the *baptism* and the *filling* of the Holy Spirit. In a sense Christ did not experience the first of these, although, as we have noted, He was born of the Holy Spirit. While He was not baptized by the Holy Spirit, we who receive Him as Saviour are. Our new birth and baptism of the Holy Spirit take place at the same time - they are 'coextensive, and it is impossible to be saved without this work of the Holy Spirit'.[8] It is this baptism which places us in the body of Christ according to Paul who says, 'For by one Spirit we were all baptized into one body' (1 Cor.

12:13). This is the baptism he refers to in Ephesians 4:5, 'One Lord, one faith, one baptism'.

Having received Christ as Saviour we are baptized into His body by the Holy Spirit; and at the same time Jesus begins to indwell us by the Holy Spirit - from the instant of our conception, in the sense of the new birth, we have the Holy Spirit (Rom. 8:9). This initial filling renders further fillings possible after the pattern of Christ who was filled from conception but at baptism experienced the coming of the Spirit upon Him in a fresh way. Professor Donald Macleod is helpful here. He says, in dealing with the meaning of the descent of the Spirit upon Christ, that

> 'The most likely possibility is that it was a fresh enduement with spiritual power granted as preparation for a critical new phase of His life. It is quite clear from the New Testament that those who have been filled with the Spirit can be filled again. Peter, for example, having already been filled at Pentecost is filled again in Acts 4:8; and in the light of Luke 12:11,12 all Christians have the right to expect that at critical moments they will receive special spiritual help.'[9]

What greater encouragement could be offered us than this example in Christ's life of the help of the Holy Spirit? While He, as God, did not require this filling, in His human nature He received it, thus showing us the way of the Spirit's working in our lives.

The meaning of the coming of the Holy Spirit upon Christ at His baptism is often overlooked by us in our materialistic and secular age. If He needed the Holy Spirit to do His work on earth then what hope have we without Him? How foolish to forfeit this power, substituting subtle theological twists and clever programmes, funds and fun - endless enticements all of which offer only 'form' and have no 'substance'!

Some very remarkable events took place at Christ's baptism. As He stood in the place of obedience, and as He prayed, the heavens were opened to Him and God responded. He was beginning a new, difficult and challenging phase of His life's work and help came to Him through an enduement of power from the Holy Spirit. At this critical point He needed the Holy Spirit. All that He did from that moment onward was marked by the Holy Spirit's ministry in His life. This is His example, it is here that we are to place our feet in following Him.

Yet how evident is the Holy Spirit in the lives of most Christians today? How slight is the teaching given regarding quenching and grieving the Spirit, how small the emphasis upon His filling. A D.I.Y. mentality seems to have invaded the church as a whole. Yet this is contrary to the whole example of our Lord. His reliance upon the Holy Spirit as He fulfilled God's righteousness on earth is our pattern for ministry. And it was only after the Spirit had descended and abode upon Him that the Father's voice of approval was heard.

(iii) 'This is My beloved Son, in whom I am well pleased.'
Three times throughout Christ's public ministry the Father spoke from heaven: first at His baptism, again at His transfiguration (Matt. 17:5) and finally just before He went to the cross (John 12:28). As His baptism implied transition from private to public ministry, His transfiguration implied transition from earthly to heavenly ministry. And as He approached Calvary all of the past and future ministry merged in His words, 'Father, glorify Your name'. Then a voice came from heaven saying, 'I have both glorified it and will glorify it again.'

Earlier in John's Gospel we read of Christ's anticipation of His death and departure from earth. He says, 'He who sent Me is with Me. The Father has not left Me alone, for I always do those things that please Him' (John 8:29). Likewise Christ has not left us alone. Before His ascension He promised, 'I will pray the Father, and He will give you another Helper, that He may abide with you forever, even the Spirit of truth, whom the world cannot receive, because it neither sees Him nor knows Him; but you know Him, for He dwells with you and will be in you' (John 14:16,17).

From conception Christ was filled with the Holy Spirit. From the instant of our new birth we too are filled with the Holy Spirit. As Christ received an enduement of the Spirit when He embarked upon His public ministry, so we too may receive an added enduement of the Spirit when needed. Central to our relationship with the Holy Spirit is obedience. Through obeying the command of grace to come to Jesus for salvation we receive life in the Spirit. Through our obedience in submitting to Him we serve in the power of the Spirit.

Jesus Christ fulfilled all righteousness, all that Heaven commanded He obeyed. And through His example we learn that obedience brings access - the heavens are opened, and obedience brings acceptance - the pleasure of the Father. To refuse water baptism is to choose disobedience. It is an important step in sanctification which brings us to greater conformity to Christ. The best way to truly please the Father is to become like the Son.

References

1. Williston Walker, *A History of The Christian Church* (Edinburgh: T.& T. Clark, 1918), pp. 93,94.

2. Charles Ryrie, *Biblical Theology of the New Testament* (Chicago: Moody Press, 1959), p. 45.

3. Warren Wiersbe, *Be Right* (Wheaton, Illinois: Victor Books, 1984), p. 17.

4. F. F. Bruce, *The Epistle To The Hebrews* (Grand Rapids, Michigan: Wm. B. Eerdmans Publishing Co., 1964), p. 104.

5. Alfred Edersheim, *The Life and Times of Jesus The Messiah* (Grand Rapids, Michigan: Associated Publishers And Authors Inc., n.d.), p. 221.

6. W. E. Vine, *An Expository Dictionary Of New Testament Words* (Westwood, New Jersey: Fleming H. Revell Company, 1966), Vol. III, p. 277.

7. John Walvoord, *The Holy Spirit* (Grand Rapids, Michigan: Zondervan Publishing House, 1954), p. 92.

8. *Ibid.* p. 139.

9. Donald Macleod, *The Spirit of Promise* (Tain, Ross-Shire, Scotland: Christian Focus Publications, 1986), p.12.

Jesus represents the only serious adversary the Devil has to reckon with, so naturally he rates special attention.

Malcolm Muggeridge, *Jesus The Man Who Lives*

Unless there is within you that which is above you, you will soon yield to that which is about you.

Author Unknown

We are living in a part of the universe occupied by the rebel. Enemy-occupied territory - that is what this world is.

C. S. Lewis, *Mere Christianity*

'Tis one thing to be tempted, Escalus, Another thing to fall.

William Shakespeare, *Measure for Measure*

For we do not have a High Priest who cannot sympathize with our weakness, but was in all points tempted as we are, yet without sin.

Hebrews 2:17,18

No temptation has overtaken you except such as is common to man; but God is faithful, who will not allow you to be tempted beyond what you are able, but with the temptation will also make the way of escape, that you may be able to bear it.

1 Corinthians 10:13

Temptations, when we first meet them, are as the lion that roared upon Samson; but if we overcome them, the next time we see them we shall find a nest of honey within them.

John Bunyan, *Sermons*

'The Divine and the devilish lie very near each other.'

4

WARFARE IN THE WILDERNESS

Immediately after Christ's baptism in the Jordan River there followed His temptation in the Judean Wilderness. Between the voice of the Father from heaven and the subtle sound of Satan's temptation there was only a brief time, at most about 40 days if the temptations came at the end of His wilderness fast.

In the preceding chapter we noted that Christ was anointed with the Holy Spirit at His baptism, receiving an enduement of power to fulfil God's purpose which began with a determined confrontation with the devil. It would be difficult to conceive of a greater contrast: enduement by the Spirit of God and enticement by Satan, all in the space of a few days. It is here, as it was at Christ's mountain top transfiguration. Immediately after it's glory He descended to the valley to be confronted by demons. There an anguished father interceded on his son's behalf and the Lord delivered him from demon possession (Matt. 17:1-18). The heights and depths of spiritual experience seem often to follow hard upon one another.

The Synoptic Gospels each contain an account of Christ's temptation. Mark offers no details, only mentioning that Christ was alone in the wilderness among wild beasts and was tempted there by Satan (Mark 1:12,13). He does, however, tell us something in a more forceful way than either Matthew or Luke. They record that Jesus was '*led* by the Spirit into the wilderness' (Matt. 4:1; Luke 4:1). But Mark states that 'the Spirit *drove* Him into the wilderness' (Mark 1:12). While this term does not suggest compulsion being exerted upon an unwilling subject, it does imply irresistible force and marks this event with a sense both of urgency and certainty.

The fact that Jesus was 'led' or 'driven' into the wilderness by the Holy Spirit is important. He was filled with the Spirit and led by Him, this leading resulting in His confrontation with Satan. Their encounter was by God's design. It was part of His plan that the Personal Saviour confront the personal devil; that 'the ruler of this world' be brought before the Christ of God, the Ruler of the universe. In this act God is the initiator, not Satan. Christ was not caught in the wilderness, cornered by Satan and tempted to worship him. Rather at the very beginning of His public ministry, He came there urgently to contend with the great enemy of our souls and to defeat him.

Christ's incarnation made this confrontation possible and this victory, as well as all those which precede and follow it, provides the reason for His coming in human form: 'Inasmuch as the children have partaken of flesh and blood, He Himself likewise shared in the same, that through death He might destroy him who had the power of death, that is, the devil' (Hebrews 2:14).

By His death Christ defeated eternal death, the devil's desire for all mankind. By His life He defeated the devil's power in temptation, affirming His deity and showing us how we may deal victoriously with temptation in our own lives. Because of Christ's coming the devil can neither destroy our souls in eternity nor defeat us in time. Christ has secured our position both on earth and in heaven.

In this chapter we will consider the meaning and nature of temptation as presented in Scripture as a whole, as well as Christ's three specific wilderness temptations. While both Matthew and Luke give detailed accounts of these temptations, as we followed Matthew's record of Christ's baptism, we will also follow his record of the temptations (Matthew 4:1-11).

Temptation in Scripture

Temptation is one of those things which, although we find it hard to define, we none-the-less know exactly what it is through personal experience. Daily we face temptations coming to us in many ways. In our increasingly secular, selfish, humanistic, dehumanizing age temptation assumes an increasing presence in our lives. One of it's most frightening features is its subtle capacity to press us into the mould of the world. This blurring of distinction between the Christian and non-Christian reduces our effectiveness in witness and presents an uncertain representation of Christ before the watching world.

A basic passage in the New Testament concerning temptation is James 1:12-15. In these verses James clarifies the difference between temptation and testing or trial, terms which often seem confusing to us. He helps us understand that while God tests or tries us, Satan tempts us. An important part of the difference between these is the intent which lies behind them. God allows, even brings, testing in order to deepen our commitment to Him and dependency upon Him, things which ultimately work for our own good. His testing can make us stronger and is designed to complete our faith and enhance our spiritual growth. Satan has altogether different intentions behind his temptations. His desire is our downfall, the development of doubt in our minds which will lead on to the destruction of our effectiveness as servants of Christ.

One of the problems we face regarding testing or temptation is that we do not always know whether an experience is from God or Satan. It is this uncertainty that creates our dilemma, and adding to it is the fact that sometimes what seems to be a test or temptation is entirely neutral. In such instances it is our response to it which moves it beyond neutrality into either sin or increased holiness in our lives.

Regarding this passage in James, one writer suggests that it's whole purpose seems to be to teach us 'that the same event can go either way; it can become a trial for strengthening you or a temptation - weakening you - depending on how you respond to it ... From God's perspective, the event is an opportunity, designed for your good; a trial that can strengthen. From Satan's perspective, the event has potential for evil that will weaken you. In every trial, you should remember the double possibility'.[1]

James 1:14, 15 especially offers insight into the working of temptation and testing in our lives: 'But each one is tempted when he is drawn away by his own devices and enticed. The, when desire has conceived, it gives birth to sin; and sin, when it is full grown, brings forth death.'

Here James isolates the key - *our desire* - which determines whether an experience will result in strengthening or weakening us. It can transform the experience into temptation and produce defeat. However, if there is within us the desire of Christ, if we are being conformed to Him in mind, heart and soul, then our resistance results in growth. If it is 'no longer I who live, but Christ lives in me' then temptations lose their power. The problem of sin is the presence of sin in our lives, we are tempted to commit outward sin because of indwelling sin. In Romans 6:12,13 Paul speaks specifically on this point, warning us:

'... do not let sin reign in your mortal body, that you should obey its lusts. And do not present your members as instruments of unrighteousness to sin, but present yourselves to God as being alive from the dead, and your members as instruments of righteousness to God.'

The Nature of Temptation

Ultimately all temptation comes from the devil, and we must never discount his presence and power in our world. However, there are various means and methods which he employs. Generally two sets of three things are suggested in clarifying temptation:

(1) the world, the flesh, and the devil;
(2) the lust of the eye, the lust of the flesh, and the pride of life.

With this in mind the following chart should be helpful in showing us the contrasting reactions to temptation between the First Adam and the Last Adam.

The World	The Flesh	The Devil
The Lust of the Eye	The Lust of the Flesh	The Pride of Life

(The First Adam - Genesis 3:1-6, the fruit appeared:)

Pleasant to the eye	Good for Food	Desirable to make one wise

(The Last Adam - Matthew 4:1-11)

The Temple Spectacle a public leap,	Transforming stones into bread	The Devil's request - 'worship me'

The First Adam yielded, accepting the devil's offer, Genesis 3:6. The Last Adam resisted, dismissing the devil, Matthew 4:10.

From the first to the last the devil is the tempter. His means and methods may vary but his intention is constant - our destruction. What the First Adam lost, the Last Adam regained, and only in Him do we have hope and help for deliverance. He teaches us to pray, 'And do not lead us into temptation, But deliver us from the evil one. For Yours is the kingdom and the power and the glory forever. Amen' (Matt. 6:13).

The Tempter - Satan

To deny the devil's reality is to deny the Bible for it is impossible to accept Scripture literally and reject a literal devil. Although some, among them theologians and church leaders, discount his literal existence, those who worship him know him to be real and have a clear understanding of his place in world affairs. Anton LaVey, founder and head of the Church of Satan, states that 'The Hebrew word, Satan, means "the opposite" or "the adversary"... It's the spirit of discovery, free-thinking rebelliousness.'[2] For LaVey and his followers the devil is not a malevolent spirit as religious modernism suggests, nor simply the symbol for the evil tendencies in human nature - the devil with the 'd' removed. For them he is the adversary of God and all He represents, just as the Bible declares him to be in I Peter 5:8. As God is a Personal Being, so is Satan. As God is the Father of believers, Satan is the father of unbelievers (John 8:41-44). And as God wants His children to be like Him so Satan works his wiles to conform his followers to his own wishes and image. [3]

It was this adversary Satan whom Christ engaged in the wilderness. And he is the same one with whom we must contend every day for he is 'the prince of this world' in which we live (John 14:30). While this does not mean that the devil controls all, it does mean that he rules the evil in the world, including all who are spiritually separated from God.

Two striking verses in Scripture which instruct us in our relationship with God and the devil are James 4:7,8: '...submit to God. Resist the devil and he will flee from you. Draw near to God and He will draw near to you.'

According to the teaching of this passage we are as near to God as we want to be, or as near to the devil as we want to be. Our ability to draw near to God rests in the blood of Christ Jesus, the symbol of His finished work (Eph. 2:13). Yet, being covered by the blood does not mean that we automatically conform to Christ. Having been chosen to salvation in Him does not mean that we need never choose for ourselves. Temptation is based upon choice - that was the point of all Christ's wilderness temptations - choice, to obey or not to obey God and His Word. Because of Christ, when we are faced with choices, we have His power and example to choose correctly.

The Tempted - Christ Jesus

Satan came to Adam and Eve in Eden to tempt them. The Last Adam, Christ Jesus, came to the wilderness and there initiated the confrontation which resulted in His temptation by Satan. As I have already stated, it was God who was the aggressor in this encounter and I agree with G. Campbell Morgan when he says, 'My own conviction is that if the devil could have escaped that day, he would have done so.'[4]

It is beyond the purpose of this chapter to discuss in detail the temptability of Christ. Yet, it is necessary to at least establish the premise from which His temptations are to be considered. Two questions present themselves to us: (i) could Christ be tempted? (ii) and could Christ have sinned? The answer to the first question is 'yes', and to the second, 'no'. Temptation requires that the tempter be sinful, but not that the tempted be. Jesus was genuinely tempted 'in all points as we are, yet without sin' (Hebrews 4:15). He neither sinned, nor could He have sinned.

This position poses a problem for some as they reason that if a person cannot sin then they cannot be tempted to sin. However, this is not necessarily so, 'any more than it would be correct to say that because an army cannot be conquered, it cannot be attacked'.[5] Just as an invincible army may be attacked, so Christ could be, and was tempted. Not only does the Bible state this as true, but our personal experience with temptation demands that it be true. Our temptations are real and for Christ's to have been anything less would have reduced them to an empty formality and Him to hypocrisy.

Why Was Christ Tempted?
We will consider the purpose for Christ's temptation in a four-fold way, each of which is of personal benefit to the Christian.

(i) First, Christ was tempted to show us that there was no sin in Him and no possibility for sin. His temptation and triumph affirms the stability of the foundation upon which our faith rests. The Christian is no more secure than the object of his faith and through temptation Christ shows us that not even the concentrated efforts of Satan can shake our foundation - Christ Jesus. Thus, this first act of His public ministry declares His absolute dominion over our adversary. Beyond any doubt He confirms to the Christian that 'He who is in you is greater than he who is in the world' (1 John 4:4). It is significant that Christ, the Last Adam, demonstrates His perfection at the point where the First Adam demonstrated his sinfulness -- at the point of temptation.

I have referred here to Christ as the Last Adam. Although He is sometimes called the Second Adam, this is His proper Biblical title. There are only two Adams in Scripture and all men live under the consequences of the acts of one of them. We are either bound by the penalty of the First Adam's sin, or liberated by the power of the Last Adam's salvation. And we are bearing the image and showing forth the life of either the First or the Last Adam; there is no alternative to this. We all stand at one of these two places.

Christ began His public ministry by placing Himself before Satan. There He stood in victory where Adam had fallen in defeat. Regarding the Christian Paul writes in 1 Corinthians 15:49 that, 'As we have borne the image of the man of dust, we shall also bear the image of the heavenly Man.' Christ's image is born in us at salvation and inherent in it is the ability to mirror His victory over temptation. Because He was victorious we may be victorious, we do not have to yield! Christ was tempted to show that nothing can shake the foundation of our faith. It is the image of the Victor that we bear and it is in His likeness we are to live, even when we are tempted.

(2) The second reason for Christ's temptation was that it enables Him to sympathize with us in ours (Heb. 4:15). He enters into our temptation with us, understanding through His experience the power it exerts upon our lives.

I like very much the wording of the Authorized Version for Hebrews 4:15 as it points out that Christ, our High Priest, is 'touched with the feeling of our infirmities'. What we feel, He feels with us. He has stood where we stand when tempted, and He won against the devil. He stands with us, feeling with us the reality of our temptation, and in His sympathetic presence is the strength for our victory.

(3) The third reason for Christ's temptation is an extension of the second. He sympathizes with us and is also able to help us when tempted. Hebrews 2:18 is a verse of great encouragement to every believer, 'For in that He Himself has suffered, being tempted, He is able to aid those who are tempted'. The Greek word for 'aid' is

boetheo and it is one of my favourite words in that language. It means that Christ is able 'to run to the cry of those in danger and bring them aid'.[6] An unknown poet has put it this way:

> With pitying eye, the Prince of grace
> Beheld our helpless grief;
> He saw, and (Oh, amazing love!)
> He ran to our relief.

There is a picture of Christ in this word. He came from heaven to rescue us from our sins, placing our feet upon His firm foundation. He continues to come to us, guarding us from the tempting power of our enemy. What delight we should take in *boetheo*, our Saviour who comes and continues to come, the King who hears our cry and runs to help us.

(4) The final reason for Christ's temptation is one which may seem obvious to us. He was tempted in order to give us an example of how to deal with our own temptations. Although this was not the primary reason for His temptations they do provide us with lessons we should learn and apply. In addition to specific lessons from His three specific temptations there are general observations which will prepare us for a closer study and application of these.

Three General Observations on Temptation

First, the Holy Spirit has a *role* in temptation. This is of vital importance and must not be missed. Luke 4:1 tells us two things, 'Jesus, being *filled with the Holy Spirit*, returned from the Jordan and was *led by the Spirit* into the wilderness'. Being filled with the Spirit is a reference to the descent of the Spirit on the Son at His baptism (Matt. 3:16). Thus filled He was then led by the Spirit into the wilderness -- the arena of confrontation and temptation. At the close of the temptations Luke tells us that 'Jesus returned in the *power of the Spirit* to Galilee' (4:14). Throughout the period of temptations Christ was filled, led and empowered by the Holy Spirit. Learning and applying this lesson will make the difference between defeat and victory in our lives. When tempted we do not stand alone, the One who has come to us in Christ's place stands with us to help us.

(2) A second observation is the *certainty* of temptation. Christ teaches His followers to pray, 'do not lead us into temptation' (Matt. 6:13). And Paul advises us to 'Put on the Lord Jesus Christ, and make no provision for the flesh, to fulfill its lusts' (Rom. 13:14). Temptation is to be avoided whenever possible, but it is not always possible!

In His Prayer of Intercession Christ says to the Father on our behalf, 'I do not pray that You should take them out of the world, but that You should keep them from the evil one' (John 17:15). The Christian is to stay here, but for us to remain in the world will inevitably mean that at times we will be tempted to become of the world. Yet, as the Holy Spirit brought Christ to the place of temptation for a purpose, so the Father allows us to remain in the world for a purpose–but just as Christ was not alone, neither are we. The effectiveness of the Christian as salt and light requires they demonstrate the ability to resist temptation, in the power of the Holy Spirit.

(3) Our final observation relates to the part *God's Word* has in the midst of temptation. As we study the wilderness temptations this becomes increasingly evident. But here it is necessary to say that knowing and doing are not the same thing. We may *know* that in resisting temptation Christ quoted Scripture - but we may never have *done* this ourselves. Very often our coming to God's Word is for the purpose of learning some new thing and not to receive power from it. Power comes when what we know is applied in life, it is then that the supernatural power of the living Word of God is released. Christ's quotation of Scripture was not the voicing of a magic formula to shield Him from the tempter's power. Rather it flowed naturally from His deep understanding of the life-context in which the words were first used. The Word was part of Him and in temptation became both armour and sword for the offence. With it He drove the devil into submission, defeated him, dismissing him from His presence.

The Wilderness Temptations

The immediate context for Christ's temptations was a fast lasting forty days and nights (Matt. 4:2). Although Jesus says little about fasting, and this is the only Biblical account we have of Him engaging in one, we should not overlook it. John Wesley's comment is worth noting, 'Some have exalted religious fasting beyond all Scripture and reason; and others have utterly disregarded it'.[7]

These are the extremes to be avoided, yet there is a Biblical balance regarding fasting which needs to be regained in contemporary Christianity. An intriguing question we should ask ourselves is this, "Are we going too fast to fast?" In our rush to be doing, have we missed being what God desires? Fasting develops spiritual character for at its foundation rests self-denial. This is linked closely with Christ's wilderness temptations as in each one the issue is obedience.

When tempted will He be ruled by self, by the expectations of others, by Satan - or by God? Ultimately who will He obey, God or another? In a later chapter we will consider two crosses, Christ's and ours. When the Lord speaks of our cross the emphasis is upon self-denial, for only as we deny ourselves will we take our cross and follow Him (Matt. 16:24). Satan and self, if unchecked, will always lead us away from obedience to Christ. In the wilderness Jesus was engaged in fasting, a spiritual discipline which teaches us to say 'no' to the demands of self, and opens before us a higher level of understanding regarding submission to God and denial of self.

The Temptations Begin - With a Word

Matthew tells us that Satan opened his attack with a word - 'if' (Matt. 4:3). He began where he always begins, with doubt, 'If You are the Son of God'. This is how he approached Eve in Eden when he asked, 'Has God indeed said 'You shall not eat of every tree of the garden' (Gen. 3:1)?' At the close of Christ's life he is heard through the voices of those surrounding the cross, 'If You are the Son of God, come down from the cross' (Matt. 27:40). The scene and time are different but the subtlety is the same - 'if'. From beginning to end a basic tactic of the devil is to create doubt in our relationship with God.

Satan deceived Eve into accepting his misconception of God as one who was withholding what was good from her. He could not deceive Christ in the same way for Jesus knew God's plan for Him involved the cross and understood that this was best for Himself and mankind. Freedom from doubt comes from knowing God who we know best through knowing of His Son. In his book *In Two Minds* Os Guinness writes that,

> 'At its most basic, doubt is a matter of truth, trust and trustworthiness. Can we trust him enough to rely on him utterly? Do we trust him enough to enjoy him? Is the whole of life different for that trust?'[8]

As our conformity to Christ increases, space in our lives for doubt decreases and as we come to radically rely upon God this certainty brings as its reward the greatest enjoyment of God. We will not enjoy him if we doubt Him.

At His baptism Jesus heard the words of the Father, 'You are My beloved Son, in whom I am well pleased' (Luke 3:22). Now He hears Satan's words announcing His first temptation, 'If You are the Son of God, command that these stones become bread' (Matt. 4:3). Satan knew that Jesus was God and Jesus knew He was God. It was not so much the tempter's design to cause Him to doubt His identity as to doubt the plan of God for His life. That plan involved pain and death. Did it have to be that way? Could the same end be secured through less demanding means? Was it essential that He suffer hunger in the wilderness and death on Golgotha? Again we remind ourselves of the essential aspects of Christ's temptations: self-denial and obedience. If we doubt God we will neither deny ourselves nor obey Him. We should always have His example before us when tempted.

The First Temptation - Matthew 4:3,4

The scene of Christ's first temptation is the Judean Wilderness and the stated temptation is to change some of the desert stones into bread. He has been fasting and is hungry and the temptation seems altogether natural. But there is more involved than just this simple act well within Christ's power to perform. The temptation which lies behind it is this: *place the material before the spiritual*. In its immediate form this meant supplying food to satisfy His hunger. In its wider sense it was to bring in God's kingdom through physical rather than spiritual means, thus subverting God's plan.

When Jesus began His public ministry times were hard. The Israelites were politically oppressed by the Romans and taxed almost beyond endurance. There was unemployment on a broad scale. In the Parable of the Vineyard Christ tells us that even at the eleventh hour men were idle in the marketplace looking for work (Matt. 20:1,9). And in John 6 we learn that 5,000 men gathered about Him - and all were without food.

When Satan said, 'Turn these stones into bread', a much greater temptation was present than just Christ's own hunger. If He did this He could feed thousands of hungry people. He was not indifferent to the physical needs of others and He never discounted the importance of bread. As He had no vices, Satan tempted Him through a virtue - His heart of compassion. If it was the Father's plan that He gain a hearing with the people, would they not surely listen if fed and content? When He later fed the 5,000 they immediately wanted to make Him king, even by force if necessary (John 6:15). An immediate kingdom lay before Him, all He had to do was change the stones into bread.

Of course this would have resulted in an earthly and material kingdom and His was to be heavenly and spiritual. It was God's plan that He do things in and through His subjects and that would require faith on their part. So long as He simply did things for them there would never be such faith.

During the Colonial era of missions, many parts of the world became filled with 'rice Christians' - those who professed conversion because of the material benefits involved. This practice did not begin nor end with that era. Many people respond to the false message of some preacher whom they believe.

Our Lord knew well the value of bread and the agony of the

father with nothing to give his hungry children, the mother's anguish at the cry of her little ones. But He also understood the priority set by Heaven and the eternal value of the soul as contrasted with the temporariness of earthly life. His own advice and example was always, 'Seek first the kingdom of God and His righteousness, and all these things shall be added to you' (Matt. 6:33).

Christ resisted the devil's temptation, responding with Deuteronomy 8:3, 'It is written, "Men shall not live by bread alone, but by every word that proceeds from the mouth of God" '. The context of this verse is God's humbling Israel through hunger for the purpose of bringing them to obedience. He tested them so they would come to trust Him, and then He gave them manna. Christ could have used His powers to run ahead of God, meeting His immediate needs and those of the multitudes. He refused the temptation to do so, applying the lesson of this Scripture, denying Himself and obeying God's Word. Because He was willing to wait for God's supply in God's time, there are several lessons we may learn from His experience.

(i) Christ had fasted, He was hungry and Satan tempted Him at this time of physical weakness. At such a time, when physically or emotionally weak, we are particularly open to temptation yet we need not yield. Christ's example shows us that even in human weakness a man filled with the Spirit of God is more than a match for the tempter!

(ii) Another lesson we may learn relates to our natural human appetites. They are neutral, neither good nor bad in themselves. We do not become hungry because of the Genesis 3 fall. Our appetites exist as an integral part of the way God has made us. Sin enters when we yield to the temptation to meet these needs in a way which violates God's will.

(iii) Our third lesson is the importance of patience. Changing stones into bread would have immediately satisfied Christ's hunger. However, He knew His need for food would be met in God's time. Matthew 4:11 tells us that at the end of the temptations 'angels came and ministered to Him'. That they supplied nourishment for

His body would have been entirely natural. Israel's waiting in their wilderness experience was rewarded with manna. God always remembers and responds, and He always does so in time.

For most of us waiting is one of the hardest things we may be asked to do. But time spent waiting on God is never time wasted nor lost. While we wait He is enlarging our souls in faith and dependence. If in haste we seek immediate solutions we forfeit the growth and blessing which accompanies patience. In our age of instant everything, Christ-like patience is sadly in decline. Patience is born of trust. G. Campbell Morgan calls it 'the flower of fidelity'.'

Christ's first temptation involved disregard for God's way and acceptance of an alternative with the aim of arriving at the same end. God's way is always based upon His order: the spiritual first and material second. Man's way is generally a reversal of this order and will never lead us to God.

The Second Temptation - Matthew 4:5-7

In Christ's second temptation the scene changes from the wilderness to the pinnacle of Herod's newly completed temple in Jerusalem. The stated temptation is, 'If You are the Son of God, throw Yourself down. For it is written; He shall give His angels charge concerning you; and in their hands they shall bear you up, lest you dash your foot against the stone' (Matt. 4:6,7; Psalm 91:11,12). It is significant that as Christ used Scripture to counter the devil's first temptation, the devil misuses Scripture to construct the second. It is also significant that there is a second temptation! Even though the first failed the devil does not give up. If he cannot succeed in tempting our vices he will attack our virtues. And if we say, 'Thus says the Lord', he becomes our echo, even turning Scripture to his own use. And as contemporary cults have clearly demonstrated, the Bible can be *made* to say anything!

Just as in the first temptation there is also in the second a more subtle aspect underlying what is stated. In this case it involves three things.

First is the appeal to do something spectacular. The pinnacle of the temple was 400 feet high. A leap from there, witnessed by the people in the courtyard below, would have insured an immediate following. First century Israel looked for their Messiah to come. They longed for him to appear, defeat their enemies and set up a kingdom on earth, one in which they would share in its power and glory. One of the final Old Testament prophecies relating to the Messiah says: 'Behold, I send My messenger, and he will prepare the way before Me. And the Lord, whom you seek, will suddenly come to His temple, even the Messenger of the covenant, in whom you delight. Behold, He is coming, says the Lord of hosts' (Mal. 3:1). The temple was newly completed and Messianic hopes ran high. To have yielded to Satan's temptation would without doubt have resulted in being acknowledged as that promised Messiah by the people. A kingdom, a following, but what kind? A spectacular leap would appeal to man's lower nature, the people might follow but not by faith, only because of sight. And those who follow the spectacular by sight never follow very long. It is the soul, not the eye, which must be won and satisfied.

In this second temptation the principle of faith hangs in the balance with Christ's decision, and along with it the whole nature of the kingdom He came to establish. It has been observed that, 'If he had fallen in with the Devil's proposal to publicize himself he would have reduced what was destined to become a universal religion to the dimensions of a cult'.[10] If those who were in the courtyard that day followed Him because of this phenomenon, what of those who did not see? Would other spectacles be demanded? Christ's kingdom is built upon the capture of our soul, not of our senses. His way is to lead us in faith and not by sight.

The second subtlety of this temptation is that it called for Christ to demonstrate presumption rather than a trusting faith in God's Word. The Bible defines faith as 'the substance of things hoped for, the evidence of things not seen' (Heb. 11:1). What is realized and visualized has nothing to do with Biblical faith. By leaping from the temple Christ would have been demanding God's intervention and rescue rather than demonstrating faith. Putting God to the test is evidence of a lack of trust. 'It is when we doubt a person that we make experiments to discover how far they are to be trusted. To make experiments of any kind with God, is to reveal the fact that one is not quite sure of Him. Trust never desires to tempt, to test, to trifle. It calmly, quietly abides in confidence.'[11]

Satan's third subtlety is, I believe, the most dangerous aspect of this temptation. He attempted to turn Christ from God's way to an alternative. If he succeeded he would keep Him from doing the Lord's work in the Lord's way. In his assessment of contemporary Christianity Francis Schaeffer writes that, 'The real problem is this: the church of the Lord Jesus Christ, individually or corporately, tending to do the Lord's work in the power of the flesh rather than of the Spirit'.[12] Would it be by a spectacular leap or by the solitude and agony of Gethsemane and ignominy of Golgotha that Christ would win the hearts of men and women? Only because He was willing to do the Lord's work in the Lord's way, regardless of the cost, is there help in time and hope in eternity for mankind. The flesh seeks ease and immediacy while the way of the Spirit may be demanding and consuming. Yet, as Christ was faced with this choice, so we too must choose to do the Lord's work in His way. There is little hindrance from Satan for those who serve in the flesh.

When faced with temptation we always respond, either accepting or resisting. As with the first temptation Christ resists, turning again to Scripture, 'You shall not tempt the Lord your God as you tempted Him in Massah' (Matt. 4:7; Deut. 6:16).

In the context of this verse Israel murmured and complained of thirst in the wilderness. Moses confronted them, 'Why do you contend with me? Why do you tempt the Lord?' (Exod. 17:2). But the people persisted in their demand, expecting another miracle like the one at Horeb when water came out of the rock. The place where they were now was named 'Massah and Meribah, because they tempted the Lord, saying, Is the Lord among us or not?' (Exod. 17:7). This is the incident Christ refers to in His reply.

God's Old Testament people doubted His presence and promise - even after Horeb, the manna and all the other miracles. Their demand, far from demonstrating faith, simply confirmed their doubt. And when Massah is mentioned in the New Testament it is used as an example of the unbelief which kept them from entering

Canaan (Heb. 3:7-12,19). To leap from the pinnacle would have gained Christ a following no more faithful than murmuring Israel.

There are at least three lessons we may learn from this temptation.

The first is that presumption and faith are not the same thing, even though the devil would have us believe that they are. The one time the word presumption appears in the New Testament it is in connection with those who are self-willed and walking according to the flesh (2 Peter 2:10). Lenski describes them as 'darers and self-pleasers'.[13] Christ's example is a trusting faith, not presumption which places demands on God before we will believe.

The second lesson is based upon our attitude toward God's Word. Christ's example teaches us that we are not to doubt the Bible. To demand that God prove His Word is to say that it is not enough that He has spoken it. Inspiration, inerrancy and infallibility are not doctrines to be proven but must be accepted by faith.

This does not mean that we are to simply place a blind, empty faith in Scripture. It means that, although history and our own experience provide ample evidence of its authenticity, we do not accept God's Word because of 'proof', but by faith. The demand for confirmation will always carry with it a further demand and such an approach to Scripture will never result in its acceptance. It is at this point that Satan's attack is repeatedly directed. In all his subtlety he tempts us to demand confirmation by our presumption.

The third lesson from this temptation has already been mentioned. It is a lesson basic to true Christianity. We must do the Lord's work in the Lord's way! Here I want to quote again Francis Schaeffer's statement and an added sentence as well. 'The real problem is this: the church of the Lord Jesus Christ, individually or corporately, tending to do the Lord's work in the power of the flesh rather than of the Spirit. The central problem is always in the midst of the people of God, not in the circumstances surrounding them.'[14]

One of Satan's desires in temptation is to influence Christians. If he can do this, it follows that he will rule our circumstances. We fall into his snare when we concentrate on the external rather than the internal. Circumstances will never cause us to conform to Christ, but our conformity to Him will shape circumstances about us. And it is only in this way that the world can be changed--from the inside out. If we work in the power of our flesh we can appeal only to the flesh of others. But if the Spirit of God exercises His power through us, then it is the spirit of others which will be touched.

It is the old cliche, 'We are to be *in* but not *of* the world'. Yet too often we are ruled by *where* we are rather than *who* we are. But the computer programmes and advertising techniques with which we replace the power of the Holy Spirit result in only influencing man's flesh but not his spirit. The degree to which Satan succeeds in influencing us to work in the power of our flesh and not the power of the Holy Spirit, to that degree he will diminish God's reality before the world. Then we become salt without savour and our light becomes darkness. The choice is always before us, God's way or ours, and the implications are infinite.

The Third Temptation - Matthew 4:8-10

For the third time the scene changes and the final temptation unfolds on an exceedingly high mountain. There Satan presents 'all the kingdoms of the world and their glory' and promises Jesus that 'All these things I will give You if You will fall down and worship me' (Matt. 4:8,9).

In the two preceding temptations Satan concealed an ulterior motive. Here, with uncharacteristic candour he boldly declares his intention - fall down and worship me! The third temptation is devil-worship.

In Isaiah 14 the prophet records the fall of Lucifer and reveals the terrible ambition behind it in the five 'I wills' of verses 12-14. The final one of these is the most frightening, 'I will be like the Most High' (v.14). This desire defines the third temptation, 'Put me in God's place in Your life'. The devil never appears unreasonable. He offers an exchange, - worship me and I will give You the kingdoms of this world and their glory. His offer is valid and undisputed by Christ for the dominion given to man was lost in the fall and Satan became, in Christ's own words, 'The ruler of this world' (John 12:31).

Although valid, what Satan offered, the Father had already promised the Son.

> "... I have set My King On My holy hill of Zion."
> "I will declare the decree:
> The Lord has said to Me,
> 'You are My Son,
> Today I have begotten You.
> Ask of Me, and I will give You
> The nations for Your inheritance,
> And the ends of the earth for Your possession ...' " (Psalm 2:6-8).

What the Father would give far surpassed what lay within the power of Satan to give. Satan offered a world corrupted and shaped by his character, an impermanent world doomed to destruction. The Father promised a world redeemed and renewed after the image and purpose of Christ, the eternal world of His new heaven and earth. Satan offered rule over fallen men where redemption could never be possible and only evil would be perpetuated. The Father offered the kingdom of the redeemed in which righteousness would rule and there would be no sin.

Temptation is a choice, and on that high mountain Satan placed a choice before the Lord. If He would bow to him a real, yet corrupted crown would be His in an instant. If He refused to bow, an eternal and uncorrupted crown would await Him - on the other side of Calvary. He must choose His kingdom, one with a cross; one without.

Christ declares His choice in His final response to Satan in the wilderness. As before He quotes from Deuteronomy, but first He says, 'Away with you, Satan!' (Matt. 4:10). For the first time during the temptations He speaks in His own authority as the Living Word in dismissing the devil. Then He calls upon the added authority of the Written Word, 'For it is written, You shall worship the Lord your God, and Him only you shall serve' (Matt. 4:10; Deut. 6:13).

Once again the context of this verse is important. It comes from the same chapter in which we find stated the Greatest Commandment, 'You shall love the Lord your God with all your heart, with all your soul, and with all your might' (Deut. 6:5). Also in this chapter are Moses' words of caution to the nation that they should neither forget God nor turn from Him to any form of idolatry (Deut. 6:12-14). The words and warnings the Father gave to His Old Testament people are those applied in the life of His New Testament Son. He will remember God, love Him and bow only to Him. To do otherwise would be a violation of His revealed Word and this He will not do.

There are several practical lessons we may learn from Christ's final temptation in the wilderness.

The first of these is that God's timing is always right - 'to every thing there is a season. A time for every purpose under heaven' (Eccl. 3:1). Following Christ's example, we live according to God's timing when we are submitted to His will, even when it is demanding and costs us greatly. His timing for Christ included the crown of thorns at Calvary before the crown of glory in heaven. He would rule the world, but not from a great mountain's height. He would receive His sceptre on the low brow of Golgotha and there establish the kingdom of eternal life by His death.

God's timing is always best. In the first temptation Christ said 'no' to Satan's method of securing bread. Yet He receive Bread, so much so that He is called 'the bread of life', and it has become the symbol of His love for us as we come in communion to His table.

In the second temptation He said 'no' to the promise of angelic intervention to save Him from harm caused by presumption. Yet the Father sent His angels and they ministered to all His needs.

In the third temptation He said 'no' to the kingdoms of this world. Yet He will receive them when 'The kingdoms of this world have become the kingdoms of our Lord and of His Christ, and He shall reign forever and ever!' (Rev. 11:15,). [15]

God's timing is always right and it is always best. If we will trust His timing and wait before Him He will enlarge and enrich our souls, though sometimes it may be through testing. And we will learn in the end that 'He has made everything beautiful in his time' (Eccl. 3:11).

The second lesson is this. We must not sacrifice the eternal on the altar of the immediate. The kingdom Satan offered Christ was even then passing away, but the kingdom God offered is eternal. Even in time we must remember eternity! A. W. Tozer has written, 'The spiritual man habitually makes eternity-judgments instead of time-judgments'.[16] He does this because a Christian's 'citizenship is in heaven' (Phil. 3:20). And, as Peter points out, we are only 'sojourners and pilgrims' on this earth (1 Peter 2:11). Every temptation seeks to erase this reality from our souls. The cliche, 'We are in the world but not of the world' is just that for many Christians - a cliche and nothing more. We still keep most of our eggs in this earthly basket.

In 1976 Dr. Francis Schaeffer's book *How Then Should We Live* was published. On its back cover were his words, 'I believe people are as they think. The choices we make in the next decade will mould irrevocably the direction of our culture ... and the lives of our children!'[17] The decade he referred to has come and gone as well as half of a second. Choices have been made by the church corporately and by Christians individually, and our culture and our children now bear the marks of those choices. Because of them the sanctity of life, marriage and the home erodes about us and the AIDS pandemic spreads. Within the church, because many have chosen to discredit the reality of God and doubt His Word, there is an increasing lack of direction.

Behind many of the choices which have been made are two 'bankrupt values' anchored firmly in time and this world - personal peace and affluence. Schaeffer defines these as follows. 'Personal peace means just to be let alone, not be troubled by the troubles of other people, whether across the world or across the city. Affluence means an overwhelming and ever-increasing prosperity - a life made up of things and more things - a success judged by an ever-higher level of material abundance'.[18] I believe Schaeffer is right and that these are the criteria underlying many of our choices.

In each of Satan's temptations his great aim was that all of human

102

history would be written without the cross of Christ. If there were no cross he would win, for it is the cross that calls men to live not only horizontally but vertically as well. Part of its radical nature is that it cuts through time and matter, lifting our gaze to God and eternity. And part of God's gift to us through the cross is that it gives us a Divine perspective on all things.

The true Christian world-view embraces time and eternity, earth and heaven, and enables us to see life from God's point of view. Again Tozer is helpful as he writes, 'The ability to weigh all things in the divine scale and place the same value upon them as God does is the mark of a Spirit-filled life'.[19] Remembering this will help us in making our choices. We must understand that our life is longer than time and that our choices affect ourselves and others for eternity.

Our next lesson is one which is clearly present, but often overlooked in a study of the third temptation. Jesus Christ and the soul of man are of infinite value. Satan understood this and was willing to exchange all the kingdoms and glory of this world for the worship of one individual - Jesus Christ. He knew Christ was worth more than the world. And because he knew this he understood the value of the human soul.

In Matthew 16:26 Christ asks, "For what is a man profited if he gains the whole world, and loses his own soul? Or what will a man give in exchange for his soul?" Our soul is worth more than this world. Its value was established at Calvary when God gave Christ in exchange for it. The devil's third temptation was based upon his knowledge that if Christ bowed to him He would not die for us. And if He did not die for us we could never live for Him in time and with Him in eternity. Satan knew that Christ and the souls of men are worth more than this world. Do we? Do we live as though this is true?

The last lesson we will draw from this temptation is learned from Christ's response, "You shall worship the Lord your God, and Him only you shall serve" (Matt. 4:10). Worship and service are one, so much so that in the mind of Christ they are 'two aspects of the same attitude'.[20] Satan tempted Christ to worship him and our Lord knew that whom we worship we serve, the one flowing from the other.

Man is created with the capacity and need for worship, and he will worship! For some it is Satan, for many it is self, but for the Christian is should be the Saviour. Although we may strongly denounce any form of Satan-worship as evil of the highest form, there is only a subtle difference between that and self-worship. Both turn men from Christ, the only One worthy of worship.

In the wilderness Satan attacked Christ as our Representative. His three temptations were of a representative nature, combining within them the lust of the flesh, the lust of the eye and the pride of life, all of which arise from our relationship with the world, the flesh and the devil. They show us that Jesus was tempted in every way just as we are, yet He did not yield, He did not sin. No part of our Lord's life is more practical than this as temptation is universal and constant in life. The temptations ceased and Luke closes his account by saying, 'Now when the devil had ended every temptation, he departed from Him until an opportune time' (Luke 4:13).

The remainder of Christ's life reveals that there were many 'opportune' times. His temptation did not begin, nor did it end in the wilderness. For 30 years He had resisted the devil, now for 40 days He stood against him in a special representative way, revealing the way to victory. During the next three years He will be tempted often - but will always win. His life confirms Paul's words to us: 'No temptation has overtaken you except such as is common to man; but God is faithful, who will not allow you to be tempted beyond what you are able, but with the temptation will also make the way of escape, that you may be able to bear it' (1 Cor. 10:13).

References

1. Jay E. Adams, *You Can Resist Temptation* (Fundamentalist Journal, Feb., 1989), p. 16.

2. Anton LaVey, *The Church of Satan* (Newsweek, Dec. 5, 1988), p. 29.

3. W. E. Vine, *An Expository Dictionary of New Testament Words* (Westwood, NJ.: Fleming H. Revell Company, 1966), pp. 38, 39.

4. G. Campbell Morgan, *The Crises Of The Christ* (London: Pickering & Inglis Ltd., n.d.), p. 114.

5. William G. T. Shedd, *Dogmatic Theology* (Nashville, Tn.: Thomas Nelson Publishers, n.d.), Vol. II, p. 336.

6. Kenneth S. Wuest, *Wuest's Word Studies Hebrews* (Grand Rapids: Wm. B. Eerdmans Publishing Company, 1947), p. 67.

7. Richard Foster, *Celebration of Discipline* (London: Hodder & Stoughton, 1980), p. 41.

8. Os Guinness, *In Two Minds* (Downers Grove, Il.: Inter Varsity Press, 1976), p. 15.

9. G. Campbell Morgan, *Letters To The Seven Churches* (London: Pickering & Inglis Ltd., n.d.), p. 59.

10. Malcolm Muggeridge, *Jesus The Man Who Lives* (Glasgow: William Collins Sons & Co. Ltd., 1975), p. 55.

11. Morgan, *The Crises Of The Christ*, p. 132.

12. Francis A. Schaeffer, *No Little People* (Downers Grove, Il.: Inter Varsity Press, 1974), p. 64.

13. R. C. H. Lenski, *The Interpretation of the Epistles of St. Peter, St. John and St. Jude* (Columbus, Oh.: Wartburg Press, 1945), p. 318.

14. Schaeffer, *op cit*, p. 64.

15. Peter Connolly, Class Lectures, Baptist Bible College, Springfield, Mo., U.S.A., 1966.

16. A. W. Tozer, *The Best of A. W. Tozer* (Eastbourne, E. Sussex: Kingsway Publications Ltd., 1983), p. 114.

17. Francis A. Schaeffer, *How Should We Then Live?* (Old Tappan, NJ: Fleming H. Revell Company, 1976), back cover.

18. Francis A. Schaeffer, *A Christian Manifesto* (Westchester, Il.: Crossways Books, 1981), p. 77.

19. Tozer, *op cit*, p. 113.

20. Morgan, *op cit*, p.140.

Happy is he whom truth teacheth directly, not by figures and passing words, but itself as it is.

Thomas a Kempis, *The Imitation of Christ*

He to whom the Eternal Word speaketh, is set free from a multitude of opinion.

Thomas a Kempis, *The Imitation of Christ*

My doctrine is not Mine, but His who sent Me.

John 7:16

Hear Me, everyone, and understand

Mark 7:14

If you believe in the Gospel what you like, and reject what you don't like; it is not the Gospel you believe, but yourself.

Augustine

Man is what he believes.

Anton Chekhov

He who repeats what he does not understand is no better than a donkey loaded with books.

Lebanese Proverb

5

CHRIST THE TEACHER

Nicodemus 'came to Jesus by night and said, Rabbi, we know that You are a teacher come from God' (John 3:2). What he heard and saw convinced him that this was true. In the incarnation Christ came as both message and Messenger – God's truth perfectly merged in word and deed. At Christ's transfiguration the Father spoke from heaven saying, 'This is My beloved Son, in whom I am well pleased. Hear Him!' (Matt. 17:5) Hear Him! This is what we must do, and what He says should be the foundation for all that we say. In an age in which more information is being given to us than we can assimilate it is essential that we learn to discriminate. What we 'hear' from Christ is essential truth for our own souls. We must hear Him always to the exclusion of His detractors, and sometimes to the exclusion of even His interpreters.

One of the most important lessons I learned as a graduate student came in an Old Testament class and had nothing to do with the Old Testament. Having written an assigned paper I presented it to the professor and soon received it back with his notations in red on the back page. One of the things he wrote was this, 'Quote properly!' He referred to a quotation I had included in the paper which was taken from a secondary source, not from the author who wrote it, but from another who quoted him. The lesson is evident. Always go to the source for your information whenever possible.

It may be more demanding to do so, but it is always the best way. The Gospels enable us to go to Christ for therein is preserved His teaching.

Divine revelation is in several forms: creation (Rom. 1:20); providence (Acts 14:17); the human conscience (Rom. 1:19; 2:14,15); the Bible (2 Tim. 3:16) and Jesus Christ (Matt. 1:23). The last two of these are uniquely the source of our knowledge of the Person and plan of God. They are the Word, as the life and teaching of the Living Word is revealed in the Written Word, and it is from this Word that we learn of redemption and the life to be lived by the redeemed. They are also the source of the most fundamental truths relative to humanity, the very basis for living. Modern man thinks that truth cannot be found, but he is wrong. Christ tells us plainly that both He and Scripture are truth (John 14:6; 17:17). Revelation, by its very nature, declares that God wants us to know, and that we can know truth.

In our quest for truth Jesus Christ is our teacher. In Ephesians 4:21, Paul contrasts the old man who walks one way with the new man who walks another. The difference between the two is that the new man has 'Learned Christ ... heard Him ... having been taught by Him, as the truth is in Jesus'. The truth, which Christ *is*, is transforming truth and entails all aspects of His life and ministry. It relates to our lostness in sin and His salvation, secured by us through faith in His finished work on the cross. It includes His tomb, emptied by His bodily resurrection, His ascension, His intercessory work in heaven in our behalf and His anticipated return to receive His own to Himself.[1] He alone is the source of this truth and when we receive Him as Saviour and Lord it is His indwelling Spirit of Truth who leads us into likeness to Him.

Christ The Teacher

Jesus spent a large part of His public ministry teaching people. Throughout Judea, Galilee and Perea He travelled teaching in synagogues, temples, boats, on mountains, in villages and cities. He taught multitudes, single individuals and His small band of disciples. From what we read in Scripture we know His teaching was oral. Only once are we told that He wrote anything, and on that occasion He merely traced a few words in the sand when dealing with the woman taken in adultery (John 8:6). He seems to have trusted His message to the minds and memories of men and women, communicating to them in the power of the Holy Spirit.

During His public ministry Christ was recognized as a teacher. His disciples as well as His enemies called Him 'rabbi', a title of respect often used when teachers were addressed.[2] As a teacher He trained others to be like Himself. He did not teach men simply to know certain things, but to be like Him. What He taught them to believe formed the basis for what He wanted them to become.

The Origin of Christ's Teaching

Christ left men in no doubt concerning the origin of what He taught. In October of about the year 29 AD He entered Jerusalem in the middle of the week-long Feast of Tabernacles, went to the temple, and began to teach. Among those gathering to hear Him were many Jews who expressed amazement at His teaching. They said, 'How does this Man know letters, having never studied?' (John 7:15). It seems He was sufficiently well known for it to be common knowledge that He had not received the conventional rabbinical training. Knowing this they considered only one other option. If He had not been taught by the rabbis, then what He said could only be His personal opinion. They failed completely to consider another possibility, certainly not the one His reply indicated. He introduced what they could not imagine, an authority much greater than their most revered rabbis. He said, 'My doctrine is not Mine, but His who sent Me ... I have not come of Myself, but He who sent Me is true, whom you do not know. But I know Him, for I am from Him, and He sent Me' (John 7:16, 29).

The Nature of Christ's Teaching

He taught with authority

Christ's authority rested in the Father. When He spoke, the authority behind His message was evident in its delivery. The epilogue to the Sermon on the Mount gives us insight into how His contemporaries rated His teaching. Hearing Him, 'The people were astonished ... for He taught as one having authority, and not as the scribes' (Matt. 7:28,29). While the scribes quoted some scholar as their authority, Christ referred to God. They talked about truth; He spoke absolute truth. He left His hearers open-mouthed by what He said. Yet this 'authority, which held the audience spell-bound was not the magic of a great reputation, but the irresistible force of a Divine message, delivered under the sense of a Divine mission'.[3] The message and mission were one as they merged in Christ Jesus, the Messenger.

He taught in simplicity

Christ was uncluttered with self-importance and the message He taught matched the Messenger in its simplicity. Mark tells us that 'the common people heard Him gladly' (Mark 12:37). While they may not have obeyed all they heard, it is certain that they understood His intent. It was from the common people that Christ selected most of His disciples, yet they came to understand the most profound truths He taught them.

Christ often brought common people to an uncommon level of understanding through the creation of word-pictures in parable form. He spoke of the Holy Spirit as wind, the soul as a pearl of great price, His own words as seeds, the unsaved as lost sheep and heaven as a wedding celebration. People knew what He taught because He helped them forge the link between the known and unknown. His aim was always not to impress but to instruct His hearers, and simplicity, whether in the form of parables or other methods, characterized His teaching.

The artlessness with which Christ taught bears slight resemblance to much that is said and written in His name today. There is a timeless simplicity surrounding His words. This quality must be recaptured if our teaching is to conform to His.

He opened men's minds

Christ made His hearers think. He did not simply tell them what to believe, but He guided them to the truth through their own thought processes. He told them enough, but not everything. He taught them to learn. John tells us that on one occasion Jesus was in Jerusalem at the Winter Feast of Dedication and a group of Jews surrounded Him and said, 'If You are the Christ, tell us plainly' (John 10:24). To their direct question He gave an indirect reply. He reminded them of what He had previously said about Himself. He referred to His works and pointed out that those who are His own know His identity (John 15:25-27). His answer probably provoked them - but it provoked them to think as well.

Quite often, when faced with a direct question, He would not give a direct answer. Instead He said enough to guide people into true and personal understanding. What we are told we may easily forget, but what we learn for ourselves becomes part of us in a far more lasting way.

Sometimes He used this technique with an added twist. This is what He did when giving the Parable of the Good Samaritan. It began with a question, 'And who is my neighbour'' (Luke 10:29)? At the end of the Parable He asks the same question again, never having given the answer Himself. Yet He has brought His hearers to the place where they can only draw the right conclusion about His identity. True teaching hasn't taken place until learning has taken place. Christ was a true teacher and people learned from Him. Their learning was based upon understanding and understanding is the foundation for conviction.

What Did Christ Teach?

Although a great deal has been written about many areas of Christ's life there is comparatively little written regarding what He taught. This is unfortunate as His teaching should be the basis for our own. Of course it is true that all of the Bible is inspired, and thus His recorded words are no more inspired than any other part of Scripture. But because they are the words of the Lord Jesus Christ – God incarnate -- they are unique since they tell us exactly what God chose to teach during His short time on our earth.

The volume and variety of Christ's teaching in the Gospels is extensive, touching on perhaps as many as 40 separate subjects.

Because of this it is necessary to be selective in this short section, as a good sized book would be required to cover all that He taught.

What Christ Taught About the Bible

Not everyone shares the same view of the Bible. Some deny its claims completely, considering it to be merely one book among many. Islam teaches that it is a book from God, but that it has been changed and corrupted by man, unlike the Qur'an. Others say that although it is not God's Word, it *contains* His Word. This view is expressed by Rudolf Bultmann in *Jesus Christ and Mythology,*

> 'The fact that the word of the Scriptures is God's Word cannot be demonstrated objectively; it is an event which happens here and now. God's Word is hidden in the Scriptures as each action of God is hidden elsewhere ... the Word of God is what it is only in the moment in which it is spoken. The Word of God is not a timeless statement but a concrete word addressed to men here and now ... It is His Word as an event, in an encounter.'[4]

While some deny, some doubt and some distort God's Word there are many who declare it to be just what it claims:

> 'All Scripture is given by inspiration of God, and is profitable for doctrine, for reproof, for correction, for instruction in righteousness, that the man of God may be complete, thoroughly equipped for every good work' (2 Tim. 3:16,17).

What Christ taught about the Bible is spread throughout the Gospels. And His beliefs, from which His teaching flows, relate to many aspects. He taught that:

(l) *The Bible is truth.* In His last long prayer recorded in Scripture He prayed to the Father on behalf of His followers, 'Sanctify them by Your truth, Your word is truth' (John 17:17).

(2) *The Bible is inerrant and infallible.*

> 'Do not think that I came to destroy the Law or the Prophets. I did not come to destroy but to fulfill. For assuredly, I say to you, till heaven and earth pass away, one joy or one tittle will by no means pass from the law till all is fulfilled' (Matt. 5:17, 18).

'And it is easier for heaven and earth to pass away than for one tittle of the law to fail' (Luke 16:17).

'...The Scripture cannot be broken' (John 10:35).

(3) *The Bible is God's eternal word*:   'Heaven and earth will pass away, but My words will by no means pass away' (Matt. 24:35).

(4) *The Bible and man's tradition are not to be confused*. 'But you say, Whoever says to his father or mother, Whatever profit you might have received from me has been dedicated to the temple -- is released from honouring his father or mother. Thus you have made the commandment of God of no effect by your tradition' (Matt. 15:5,6).

(5) *The Old Testament, often the target of attack, He clearly regarded as God's Word*. Christ quoted from or made direct reference to 19 Old Testament books: Genesis, Exodus, Leviticus, Numbers, Deuteronomy, I Samuel, 1 & 2 Kings, 2 Chronicles, Psalms, Isaiah, Jeremiah, Daniel, Hosea, Joel, Jonah, Micah, Zechariah and Malachi.

Of great importance in expressing His view of Scripture is the fact that Christ incorporated some of the most frequently criticized portions of the Old Testament today, into His teaching: (a) The creation of man, Matthew 19:4, Mark 10:6; (b) Noah and the Genesis flood, Matthew 24:38, 39; (c) The destruction of Sodom and Gomorrah, Matthew 10:15, Luke 17:28,29; (d) Lot's wife, Luke 17:32; (e) God's appearance to Moses in the burning bush, Mark 12:26, Luke 20:37; (f) Jonah and the great fish, Matthew 12:39-41, Luke 11:30,32.

As significant as what He said about the Bible is what He did not say. In all His teaching there is no hint of caution or warning expressed concerning supposed errors or contradictions. He referred to the Old Testament as a factual and true record of events expressing Divine truth. This is of special value in light of the Old Testament accounts He used in teaching. In our day Karl Barth has called Genesis 1-3 saga or legend and Emil Brunner has written that it is an 'existential' statement. But Christ acknowledged it as an historical statement concerning origins that is true and reliable.

113

Christ knew God's Word and based His teaching upon it. It was His knowledge that astonished the temple teachers when He visited Jerusalem at the age of 12. And about 20 years later, following His resurrection, it was this knowledge which enthralled the two disciples walking with Him to Emmaus, as 'Beginning at Moses and all the Prophets, He expounded to them in all the Scriptures the things concerning Himself' (Luke 24:27). He knew the Word of God and understood Himself as its prophetic fulfilment, that truth which lies at the heart of the New Testament.

Few things Christ taught are more important than what He said about the Bible. His view of Scripture is critical to every generation for if it is lost the link by which the Holy Spirit leads men to Christ and into His likeness is lost. We will never be like Him unless we believe as He did, and our belief is based upon God's Revelation to mankind.

Half a century ago G. Campbell Morgan felt compelled to give a public lecture stating his convictions and position on Christ and Scripture. In his closing remarks he gave this warning.

> 'I do ... most unhesitatingly affirm that the Christ presented in what is popularly known as "Modernism" is not the true Christ of the New Testament.
>
> 'I am convinced that sooner or later it will be well for all of us that we understand clearly that the true line of division between us is created by our attitude to the Bible ... The hour has surely come for the formation of a new covenant of such as accept the authority of the Christ of the New Testament, and therefore of the Bible, as final.'[5]

Less than a decade ago Francis Schaeffer again sounded a similar warning.

> 'Because of the widely accepted existential methodology in certain parts of the evangelical community, the old words *infallibility*, *inerrancy* and *without error* are meaningless today unless some phrase is added such as: the Bible is without error not only when it speaks of values, the meaning system, and religious things, but it is also without error when it speaks of history and the cosmos. If some

such phrase is not added, these words today are meaningless. It should be especially noted that the word *infallibility* is used today by men who do not apply it to the whole of Scripture, but only to the meaning system, to the value system, and certain religious things, leaving out any place where the Bible speaks of history and the things which would interest science ... I would ask again, Does inerrancy really make a difference - in the way we live our lives across the whole spectrum of human existence? Sadly we must say that we evangelicals who truly hold to the full authority of Scripture have not always done well in this respect. I have said that inerrancy is the watershed of the evangelical world. But it is not just a theological debating point. *It is the obeying of the Scripture which is the watershed, it is believing and applying it to our lives* which demonstrate whether we in fact believe it.'[6]

The day G. Campbell Morgan envisioned is upon us and Dr. Schaeffer's plea is more relevant than when he made it. In Luke 11:28 Christ said to the disciples, "Blessed are those who hear the word of God and keep it."

This is what is required if we are to be like Him.

What Christ Taught About Himself

In his book, *But That I Can't Believe!*, Bishop John A. T. Robinson asks, 'What kind of person do you think Jesus really was? A miracle-monger, a magic-man, a god in human clothes who could have done anything he liked; if he'd really wanted to?"

Robinson's novel terminology is simply the 20th century phrasing of a 1st century question. Herod said it then in this way, 'John I have beheaded, but who is this of whom I hear such things?' (Luke 9:9) Christ's disciples raised this same question also. While learning about Him, adjusting to His unpredictability and uniqueness, one day on a newly calmed sea, stilled by His word, they asked, 'Who can this be?' (Luke 8:25) And wherever He went people asked, 'Who is this Son of Man?' (John 12:34) It is a question asked across 20 centuries, and a question deserving consideration by everyone.

Throughout His public ministry Jesus taught many things

about Himself. Of all that He said His most compelling statements concerned His equality with God. He said, 'I and My Father are one' and 'He who has seen Me has seen the Father' (John 10:30; 14:9). From this we conclude that 'The character of Jesus is the character of Almighty God, the holiness of Jesus the holiness of God, the wrath of Jesus the wrath of God, the compassion of Jesus the compassion of God, the Cross of Jesus the revelation of the sorrow and self-sacrificing love with which the sin of man fills the heart of the Eternal.'[8]

His Titles

Frequently Christ referred to Himself by various titles, each of which disclosed a facet of His full identity and earthly purpose. The one He used most often was *Son of Man*. Of the more than 80 times this title is found in the Gospels, in nearly every instance it is used by Christ. It is His 'Own description of Himself, and it is the term that links Him to humanity, shows His intimate and positive relationship to the human race'.[9] Another title He employed was *Son of God* (John 5:25). Through the use of these two He identified Himself as God and man. Although He used this title less frequently, He accepted it on the numerous occasions when it was used by others in reference to Himself (e.g. Mark 14:61; Luke 22:20).

In John 4:25,26 He identifies Himself as the *Messiah*, thus the Anointed One of God, His promised deliverer for mankind. And in Luke 9:56 He assumes the identity of *Saviour*. The Hebrews did not think of this as a title, but as an activity of God. Yet in the Christian era it came to be applied to Christ in a special sense. Before His birth it was announced that He would come to save His people from their sins (Matt. 1:21). At His birth He was called the Saviour (Luke 2:11), and during His public ministry He used this title to declare His purpose on earth (Luke 19:9,10).

He is Indispensable to True Life

In addition to the titles by which He affirms His identity, He also teaches that He is indispensable to true life. This applies to all men for He alone provides access to spiritual life and the abundant life which characterizes it (John 10:10). Christ is indispensable *for* salvation and for *following* Him after salvation. In John 15:5 He says, 'Without Me you can do nothing.' This bold, but true statement is addressed to believers. Its antithesis is presented by Paul in Philippians 4:13, 'I can do all things through Christ who strengthens me'. All He asks us to do can be accomplished in His strength. He is indispensable, yet always available! The more we learn of Him and grow to be like Him, the more we understand how essential He is to true life.

John tells us of certain Greeks who came to worship at the Passover. While they were there they said to Philip, 'Sir, we wish to see Jesus' (John 12:21). They wanted to see Him in person. Of course, for us, this is impossible. However, He has given us a self-portrait, revealing His eternal identity beyond the physical and in the realm of the spiritual. Seeing Him in Scripture enables us to experience what John Bunyan writes of in his second great allegory, *The Holy War*. In it he tells of a feast given for the town of Mansoul. There were many dishes set before the people, each one representing a promise of God. And then when the feast was over, there followed entertainment presented in the form of riddles. Each riddle, when solved, disclosed something of the nature of King Shaddai and Emmanuel, His Son. Bunyan writes that through these the people were 'lightened' and saw what had never been seen before, beholding 'a kind of portraiture, and that of Emmanuel himself'.[10]

What Bunyan teaches through allegory, Christ teaches by Divine revelation in the Gospels, revealing a portrait of Himself sufficient to show that He is indispensable to true life. Among the metaphors He uses to make this revelation are these: (1) Physician, Matthew 9:12; (2) The Strong Man, Luke 11:21,22; (3) The Bread of Life, John 6:35; (4) The Light of the World, John 8:12; (5) The Door, John 10:9; (6) The Good Shepherd, John 10:11; (7) The Resurrection and the Life, John 11:25; (8) The Lord, John 13:13; (9) The Way, the Truth and the Life, our only access to the Father, John 14:6; (10) The Vine, John 15:1; (11) The King, John 18:36.

117

He teaches us that He is all of these and more. If His words, 'Without Me you can do nothing' suggest desolation, the antithesis - what can be done with Him, suggests elation!

His Authority

Because of who Christ is He possesses supreme authority. Frequently the Old Testament prophets said, 'The Lord said', but Christ says, "I say unto you" (e.g. Jer. 1:9; Matt. 5:21,22). And when He speaks in the New Testament He states His authority to do what only God can do. In His teaching He announces His power: (1) To give life, John 5:21,25; (2) To forgive sin, Matthew 9:6; Mark 2:5,10; (3) To give eternal life, John 10:27,28; (4) To heal the physical body, Mark 2:11.

In giving the Great Commission Christ declares categorically, 'All authority has been given to Me in heaven and on earth' (Matt. 28:18). It is autonomy rather than authority that many seek today. Since a Christ beyond their control is a fearful concept, men seek to create Him in their image. Many seek a religion which they can rule, rather than a Christ who is Ruler of all things.

Every effort on man's part to put aside the authority of Christ ends only in greater bondage. It is man's fundamental misunderstanding regarding freedom that causes him to interpret it as doing what he wants to do, rather than what he ought to do. Man's wants, of themselves, are slavery, leading to greater enslavement. It is obedience to Christ that liberates. He taught, 'Therefore if the Son makes you free, you shall be free indeed' (John 8:36). The words of the blind poet, George Matheson express this beautifully:

Make me a captive, Lord
  And then I shall be free;
Force me to render up my sword,
  And I shall conqueror be.
I sink in life's alarms
  When by myself I stand;
Imprison me within thine arms,
  And strong shall be my hand.'

His Purpose

Christ's purpose is summed up in the words of the prophet Isaiah which He quoted in Luke 4:18,19: 'The Spirit of the Lord is upon Me, because He has anointed Me to preach the gospel to the poor. He has sent me to heal the brokenhearted, to preach deliverance to the captives and recovery of sight to the blind, to set at liberty those who are oppressed, to preach the acceptable year of the Lord. Much of His message dealt with deliverance from bondage, a deliverance that could be accomplished only by His authority as God.

At various times throughout His ministry Christ made statements regarding His purpose on earth. Central to this was His preaching of the kingdom of God (Luke 4:43). In this statement there is combined both method and message. The method is preaching. Much of contemporary preaching has evolved to suit the preference of the hearer for a mild homily. This is far removed from what Christ did. He said that He came to *kerusso* - to herald or proclaim His message (Matt. 4:17; Mark 1:38; Luke 4:18). He came to cry out from His heart to the hearts of men. E. M. Bounds has said, 'Dead men give out dead sermons, and dead sermons kill'.[11] By contrast Christ's preaching flowed from life and brought life to those who received it.

He stated that His message concerned the kingdom of God. In a real sense this is the central message of the Bible. It is 'The Book of the Coming Kingdom of God'. And Christ presented Himself as the Eternal King, apart from whom there could be no kingdom as it rests upon Himself, the Lamb slain from the foundation of the world.[12] He had a message to give, eternal life in the Kingdom of God which was certainly to come. And He gave His message in the unction and power of the Spirit of God, for He understood fully that He was preaching life to dead men.

His Future

Christ taught His resurrection and second coming. In Galilee He told the disciples that 'The Son of Man is about to be betrayed into the hands of men, and they will kill Him, and the third day He will be raised up' (Matt. 17:22,23). He taught that after His death He

119

would rise again, and after His ascension He would return to earth again. Before the Sanhedrin, on the night of His betrayal, He said, 'Hereafter you will see the Son of Man sitting at the right hand of the Power, and coming on the clouds of heaven' (Matt. 26:64).

There was a directness and simplicity about Christ's teaching concerning Himself. He did not present Himself as a 'miracle-monger' or a 'magic-man', although in the Gospels, more than 30 of His miracles are recorded. He did say that He was God; and He spoke with the authority of God, declaring that His words were true and contained the spirit of eternal life. He said many things which made sense only because He said them, and what He taught generally had one of three effects on His hearers: 'Hatred - Terror - Adoration. There was no trace of people expressing mild approval'.[13]

This is no longer true. Twenty centuries have produced a profound change and the contemporary Christ proclaimed by many is one of whom 'mild approval' is acceptable. This is because His identity is overlaid with man's interpretations of who He is, and because His teaching has been spiritualized, demythologized and ultimately secularized. Today's Jesus is of human design and, as a consequence, very little change in people is required in order to be like him.

C. S. Lewis turns Bishop Robinson's question in the right direction. 'What are we to make of Christ? There is no question of what we can make of Him, it is entirely a question of what He intends to make of us.'[14] If we are committed to the Living and Written Word we will make of Him only what He makes of Himself -- and all that He makes of Himself. Unless we do this He will never make much of us. We can never be like Him if we do not believe what He said about Himself.

What Christ taught About God

Shirley MacLaine expresses her view of the New Age when she says, 'I am God, because all energy is plugged into the same source. We are all individualized reflections of the God Source. God is us and we are God.'[15]

Shirley MacLaine says she, and we, are God. Christ said that no one knows the 'Father except the Son, and he to whom the Son wills to reveal Him' (Matt. 11:27). And then He extends an invitation to us. 'Come to Me ... Take My yoke upon you and learn from Me' (Matt. 11:28,29). From Christ we can learn who God is, what He is like and what His plan is for man. He is the only way to the Father (John 14:6). Miss MacLaine would have us believe that there is nowhere to go, that when we sit on our chairs we are already there, that we are God.

God is Spirit

What Christ teaches about God is summed up by His statement in John 4:24 that 'God is Spirit, and those who worship Him must worship in spirit and truth'. The link between man and God is the God-Man, Christ Jesus, who took human form, enabling us to learn from Him the truth about God--to see the invisible, to handle and hear the otherwise intangible and inaudible.

John 4:24 is critical for our understanding Christ's teaching on God. Herbert Lockyer is helpful in his comments on it. He says that

> 'The link between human nature and the divine is in the human spirit, which in the believer is the shrine of the Holy Spirit (1 Cor. 6:19). All true approach to God must therefore be in spirit (Eph. 6:18). The first feature marks the intensity of this worship; while the second, in truth, the corollary of the first, is expressive of the inward character of worship coming from a spirit in harmony with the nature of the one worshipped.'[16]

God's Power is Supreme

Among the additional things we learn about God from our Lord is that His power is supreme. With Him, says the Son, 'All things are possible' for He 'is greater than all' (Matt. 19:26; John 10:29). Today it seems that 'We hardly calculate on God as a factor; we omit Him. Jesus did not. God's rule is over all; and in all our perplexity, doubt and fear, Jesus reminds us that the first thing is faith in God ... The Father is supreme. But that has more aspects than one. If our Father is supreme for us, He is supreme over us'.[17]

It is this later point we often overlook. We are delighted to announce His supremacy over our enemies, yet prone to ignore His rule in our own lives. Taking what Christ taught through His earthly example we must always bow before God, doing His will, teaching His doctrine and seeking to please Him.

God is Love

Christ also taught that God is love; the message He stated so simply in John 3:16. It is the message He illustrated often through His parables, such as that of the Two Debtors in Luke 7:41-43 and those of the Lost Sheep, Lost Coin and Lost Son in Luke 15:3-32.

Christ characterizes God's love as seeking and giving. In a special and personal sense it is experienced by the believer in redemption. Yet He also teaches that God 'makes His sun to rise on the evil and on the good' (Matt. 5:45). In His instruction that we must love our enemies, give to all who ask and refuse to ask back what has been taken from us, He uses the Father as the example we are to follow as 'He is kind to the unthankful and evil' (Luke 6:27-36).

God's love is infinite and even when reduced for finite comprehension to the form of Christ, through whom it is perfectly expressed, it remains past finding out. However, what we may discover of it is taught us by Christ through His life and teachings.

What Christ taught About the Holy Spirit

In chapter 3 we noted the special relationship existing between Christ and the Holy Spirit. There we observed that: (i) Christ was born of the Holy Spirit, Matthew 1:20; (ii) He was filled with the Holy Spirit without measure, Matthew 3:16; John 3:3,4; (iii) He was led by the Holy Spirit, Luke 4:1,2; (iv) And He rejoiced in the Holy Spirit, Luke 10:21. As would be expected, Christ, having such a relationship with the Spirit while on earth, naturally spoke often of Him during this time.

In the Bible Christ is one among many who teach about the Spirit, yet what He says is foundational. Scattered throughout His public ministry and recorded in the four Gospels are frequent references to the Spirit, and when they are combined they are a comprehensive statement of who He is and what He does. There are two basic facts upon which Christ establishes His teaching on the Holy Spirit.

The Holy Spirit is God

First is the fact of His Deity - He is God the Holy Spirit. In the Bible there are 16 titles for the Holy Spirit showing His relationship to the other members of the Trinity. Of these, 11 relate to the Father and 5 to the Son.[18] Although Christ does not use all of these, He does call Him 'the Spirit of (the) Father' and 'the Spirit of God' (Matt. 10:20; 12:28). Also, in His statement of the Great Commission He teaches the Spirit's equality with Himself as well as with the Father as He instructs us to 'make disciples of all nations, baptizing them in the name of the Father and of the Son and of the Holy Spirit' (Matt. 28:19). In this unique statement there is a nuance we should not overlook. It is that 'The use of the singular, *name*, seems to mean that the full name of deity is Father, Son, and Holy Spirit'.[19] It is significant that this is the way Christ chose to refer to the Trinity, clearly expressing the oneness of the Three.

In addition to this, Christ also emphasizes the Spirit's deity through many acts which He attributes to Him, frequently referring to things He does which can only be done by God. These will be listed later in this section.

The Holy Spirit is a Person

The second fact underlying Christ's teaching on the Holy Spirit is that He is a 'He' and not an 'it' - the Holy Spirit is a person. He describes Him as possessing the elements of personality. He does what a person, not a power or impersonal emanation from God could do. For example, He teaches, guides and communicates. These and other similar activities will also be considered later in this section, but it is important for us to understand at this point that the One who comes to us in Christ's place is a person, just as He is. 'He is *another* Helper, not a *different* Helper. The word *another* indicates *one like Himself*.'[20] The intimate personal relationship possible between God and man did not end at the ascension, rather it extends into our present moment in time through the ministry of the Holy Spirit.

It is clear from Christ's teaching that He believed the Holy Spirit to be both Divine and a person. Upon this premise He based His doctrine of the Holy Spirit. And what He taught is fundamental to our understanding of this doctrine and may be considered under the following headings.

(i) The Holy Spirit is instrumental in the inspiration of Scripture. In Mark 12:36 Christ refers to the way the human authors of the Old Testament were inspired, 'For David himself *said* by the Holy Spirit' (cf Matt. 22:43 and Psalm 110:1). This is what Peter teaches as he writes that 'Prophecy never came by the will of man, but holy men of God *spoke* as they were moved by the Holy Spirit' (2 Peter 1:21).

(ii) The Holy Spirit comes in Christ's place. The person of the Holy Spirit takes the place of the person of Jesus Christ. He is with us at Christ's request and is given to us by both Himself and the Father (John 14:16,26; 16:7).

Christ also taught about the timing of the Spirit's coming, linking it to His own departure. He told the disciples that 'It is to your advantage that I go away; for if I do not go away, the Helper will not come to you' (John 16:7). To this He added that the Spirit would come only after His own glorification, following His death and resurrection. After His resurrection He again came to the disciples and 'breathed on them, and said to them, Receive the Holy Spirit' (John 20:22). This may have been 'a temporary filling of the Spirit ... to provide for their spiritual needs prior to Pentecost'.[21] Or it may simply have been in preparation for what took place at Pentecost, for He also said, 'Behold I send the Promise of My Father upon you; but tarry in the city of Jerusalem until you are endued with power from on high' (Luke 24:49). In any event, the promise was fulfilled and the Holy Spirit came to indwell all believers at the moment of their conversion. Christ's presence is with us personally through the Holy Spirit. In John 14:18 He promised, 'I will come to you,' and in John 16:7 He said, 'I will send Him to you.'

(iii) The Holy Spirit has a ministry among men in general. Christ taught that this ministry involved convicting men of their sin (John 16:8). In a special sense He presented Him as the Agent of salvation. It is this aspect of His ministry that Christ stressed in His conversation with Nicodemus, telling him that he must be 'born again' and explaining this new birth as the function of the Holy Spirit (John 3:3,5,6).

When Christ spoke to Nicodemus about the new birth He also taught him something of the mystery of the Spirit's work in regeneration. He told him, 'The wind blows where it wishes, and you hear the sound of it, but cannot tell where it comes from or where it goes. So is everyone who is born of the Spirit' (John 3:8). That Christ intends a comparison between the wind and the working of the Spirit is indicated by the word 'so'. As the wind is both independent of man and invisible to him, so is the Holy Spirit. And as the operation of the wind is sovereign, so is that of the Spirit.

In this way Christ taught the legalist Nicodemus that the new birth is not achieved by something we do, rather by something the Spirit of God does. As Godet says, 'All is done, and nothing has been visible. What a contrast with the noisy and pompous appearance of the divine kingdom according to the Pharisaic programme'.[22] To this we might add - that of any programme devised by men!

(iv) The Holy Spirit has a ministry among Christians in particular. A great deal of what Christ teaches about the Holy Spirit is related to His ministry to believers since they are the ones He indwells and with whom He abides forever (John 14:16,17).

Christ speaks of the Spirit as 'Helper', or, as it is in the Authorized Version, 'Comforter'. This is a familiar term describing a function of the Spirit which should be more realised by us than perhaps it is. The Greek word is *Paraclete* and means one who is called to come to the side of another in order to help them. In this capacity the Spirit does give comfort, but He also gives help in a variety of ways.

It is in this context that Christ sometimes calls Him the 'Spirit of truth' (John 14:17; 16:13). He tells us that another part of His ministry is to teach us all things and to bring to our remembrance all that He has taught (John 14:26). Closely connected to this is His ability to guide us into all truth (John 16:13). Christ relates this in a very practical way to the disciples. As He warns them of persecution He also offers this consolation, 'But when they deliver you up, do not worry about how or what you should speak. For it will be given to you in that hour what you should speak; for it is not you who speak, but the Spirit of your Father who speaks in you' (Matt. 10:19,20). At such critical and emotionally charged times, the indwelling Holy Spirit will remind them of what they have learned, enabling them to give a true confession of Christ and their faith.

Christ teaches that not only may we rely upon the Spirit's help in trying times, but that through Him we have help in our witnessing at all times. In Luke 24:49 He tells the apostles to 'Tarry in the city of Jerusalem until you are endued with power from on high.' This enduement is the fulfilment of His promise concerning the coming of the Spirit. And its purpose is realized in obedience to the Great Commission to 'Go ... and make disciples of all nations' (Matt. 28:18-20). As Christ was endued with the Spirit's power to go into the wilderness to confront the devil, so the Christian is equipped by His power to go into the wilderness of this world and render effective service.

(v) The Holy Spirit always glorifies Jesus Christ (John 16:14). There is no hint of self-promotion in His ministry. As the Agent of salvation He points men to Christ the Saviour, and as the 'Spirit of truth' He directs us to Christ who is the Word of Truth incarnate (John 1:1; 14:6). He always honours Him. It is from Christ that we are taught the terrible and eternal danger of blaspheming the Holy Spirit.

Each of the Synoptic Gospels contain Christ's teaching on this sin. In Matthew 12:31,32 and Mark 3:28,29 His comments on the subject come in the context of the scribes' and Pharisees' accusations that He casts out demons by Satan's power. This was part of His teaching in Galilee and later, in Judea, He again refers to it in Luke 12:10-12. In all three cases He declares blasphemy of the Holy Spirit to be a sin beyond forgiveness. He does this because to attribute His power to the devil is implied denial of His deity. It is to say that He has no power of His own to use in this way and that He is demon-possessed.

B. B. Warfield observes that 'Because they accused Him of being possessed by an unclean spirit, He thus in awe-inspiring words warns that the blasphemy against that Spirit which is holiness itself, by whom He was really informed, is an eternally unforgivable sin ... thus the Holy Spirit is set over against God in general and blasphemy against the Holy Spirit is declared more unpardonable than general blasphemy against God ... The reason for this seems to reside in the fact that the holiness of God is especially manifested in the Holy Spirit.'[23]

The Spirit of God glorifies the Son of God and He in turn teaches a high view of the Spirit. This is significant in our day in which extravagant claims and promises are made in the name of the Holy Spirit. On the basis of Christ's teaching we must accept as truth only those things about Him of which we may say, the Spirit of truth has led us to them, taught them to us, and by them Christ alone is glorified.

What Christ Taught About Sin and Salvation

The final area of Christ's teaching to be considered is what He said about sin and salvation. In Genesis three we are introduced to both of these subjects in relation to man's temptation and fall. Sin entered because of a deliberate choice to turn from God to Satan. Even so the amazing grace of God promised a Saviour who would, by His coming, defeat both Satan and sin.

Sin is one of the most obvious facts of human behaviour. Everyone believes something about it whether they call it sin or something else. From the East we have the words of Zen master Yun-Men: 'If you want to get the plain truth, be not concerned with right and wrong. The conflict between right and wrong is the sickness of the mind.'[24] We also have the teaching of Hinduism which identifies sin as *avidya*, ignorance of truth, or maya, the feeling of individuality.[25]

In the West Kierkegaard repeatedly called it the qualitative leap which 'no science has explained nor can explain ... By the qualitative leap sin came into the world, and in this way is continually coming into it'.[26] Equally as disturbing is the teaching of situation ethics which, by denying absolutes and recognizing only principles, eliminates the possibility of sin in the sense of something being wrong.

Even the theologians have not been silent on this subject. Liberation theology implies that sin is injustice and exploitation of one group by another. It advocates a Political Messiah whose salvation is liberation from social, political and economic problems.

The list of those with something to say about sin seems endless. Everyone is concerned about sin, by whatever name it is identified. Along with concern for sin is concern for salvation, some means of righting the universal wrong. But what is sin? The way we answer this question determines our understanding of salvation.

What Christ Taught About Sin

Christ seldom spoke of sins in the plural, rather much of what He said related to sin in the singular. His emphasis was that sin is something man is, instead of various things he does. He focused on the inwardness of sin, its origin in the heart of man. In Matthew 15:11,18,19 He teaches that 'Not what goes into the mouth defiles a man; but what comes out of the mouth, this defiles a man ... those things which proceed out of the mouth come from the heart, and they defile a man. For out of the heart proceed evil thoughts, murders, adulteries, fornications, thefts, false witness, blasphemies'.

This is the concept He stresses in the Sermon on the Mount. When the Pharisees were congratulating themselves because they had never committed murder or adultery, Christ shattered their self-righteousness by saying, 'You have heard that it is said to those of old, You shall not murder, and whoever murders will be in danger of the judgment. But I say to you that whoever is angry with his brother without a cause shall be in danger of the judgment .. .you have heard that it was said to those of old, You shall not commit adultery. But I say to you that whoever looks at a woman to lust for her has already committed adultery with her in his heart' (Matt. 5:21,22, 27, 28). Christ taught that sin is an inward matter, a true affair of the heart. Sins arise from the sin within and will decrease or cease only as the old man becomes new in Christ Jesus.

In the course of His teaching on sin Christ used seven different words. Of these seven the two He used most often are:

(i) *Poneros*, or 'evil', relating to the innate depravity of man, his 'evil disposition of mind'.[27] This is the word He uses in Luke 6:45: 'A good man out of the good treasure of his heart brings forth good; and an evil man out of the evil treasure of his heart brings forth evil. For out of the abundance of the heart the mouth speaks'. Poneros stresses the inwardness of sin which lies in the heart of all men and at the heart of all sins.

(ii) amartia, 'sin', in English, and the word used most frequently in the New Testament for sin. Its literal meaning is 'to miss a mark; to be in error'.[28] Christ uses this word in John 8:34: 'Most assuredly, I say to you, whoever commits sin is a slave to sin'. By this Christ teaches that the man who lives without divine forgiveness is certainly not free for he is ruled by Satan through sin. This is a servitude without a hint of grace; a bondage which he cannot break by himself.

It is typical of His grace that very often when He uses this word it is in the context of forgiveness and deliverance from the power, penalty and presence of sin. *Amartia* and grace figure prominently in Christ's overall teaching on this subject and in general what He taught may be considered under the following headings.

(i) Man is personally responsible for his sin. Christ makes this plain in His remarks to the Pharisees in John 9:41: 'If you were blind, you would have no sin; but now you say, We see. Therefore your sin remains.' He teaches this same truth to the disciples saying, 'If I had not come and spoken to them, they would have no sin, but now they have no excuse for their sin' (John 15:22). In this way 'He declared to the Pharisees that sin is disobedience to light. He declared to His disciples when interpreting the fact of sin in the case of the Pharisees that He Himself had come into the world as light, that in His presence men saw; and that sin therefore consisted in their disobedience to the light which He granted them'.[29]

The responsibility for sin rests with all men because of the universal communication of God's truth to them: through creation (Rom. 1:20), providence (Acts 14:17), human conscience (Rom. 1:19); 2:14,15), and especially through the Living and Written Word, Christ and the Bible (John 1:14; 17:17). This universal responsibility is borne out by what John the Baptist said of Christ: 'In Him was life, and the life was the light of men ... That was the true Light which gives light to every man who comes into the world' (John 1:4,9).

(ii) Sin has power to enslave men. Perhaps the most frightening form of slavery is that which is unrecognized. We will never seek deliverance from a bondage we do not acknowledge. In John 8:31-32, Christ is speaking to a group of Jews about true freedom: 'If you abide in My word, you are My disciples indeed. And you shall know the truth, and the truth shall make you free' (John 8:31,32). To this they reply, 'We are Abraham's descendants, and have never been in bondage to anyone. How can You say, You will be made free?' The Jews spoke of hereditary freedom, Christ spoke of the bondage of sin intrinsic in the nature of every man. Having stated their bondage, He then points them to the only source of true freedom, 'If the Son makes you free, you shall be free indeed' (John 8:36).

What Christ Taught About Salvation

Christ never spoke of saving anything but humanity. We speak about saving time and things, but He never used the term in this way. The focus of His salvation was always the human soul.

As confusing as what man says of sin are his remarks on salvation. For the Hindu it is *samsara*, the transmigration of the soul, a theme taken up and Westernized by advocates of the New Age Movement. The Hare Krishna devotees are told and teach that 'Just hearing Hare Krisna, Hare Krisna, Krisna Krisna, Hare Hare/ Hare Rama, Hare Rama, Rama Rama, Hare Hare will save us'.[30] This false teaching is presented on many of our streets today. Less exotic but equally as lethal is the teaching heard from many pulpits that sincerity will see us through; that all roads do lead to heaven.

Christ's teaching on salvation is so clear that deliberate effort is required to mis-understand it. He said that He is the one way by which men may come to the Father (John 14:6), and that the means of coming, the way of salvation, is through belief in Him. He explained it to Nicodemus by saying that 'God did not send His Son into the world to condemn the world, but that the world through Him might be saved. He who believes in Him is not condemned; but he who does not believe is condemned already, because he has not believed in the name of the only begotten Son of God' (John 3:17,18). To the eternally questioning Pharisees He said, 'Therefore I said to you that you will die in your sins; for if you do not believe that I am He, you will die in your sins' (John 8:24).

Christ stressed that men must believe in Him to be saved. The belief He demands is based upon evidence, and this, in turn, He teaches is based upon two things.

(i) His word. The centrality of His word is stressed by what He said in John 5:24: 'Most assuredly, I say to you, he who hears My word and believes in Him who sent Me has everlasting life, and shall not come into judgment, but has passed from death into life.'

Because His word is vital to salvation it is targeted by the enemy. Christ warns of this in the Parable of the Sower:

'Now the parable is this: The seed is the word of God. Those by the wayside are the ones who hear; then the devil comes and takes away the word out of their hearts, lest they should believe and be saved' (Luke 8:11,12).

(ii) His works. In the Bible we have Christ's word and a record of His works by which His identity and the truth of His word are affirmed. He taught, 'The works that I do in My Father's name, they bear witness of Me ... Believe the works, that you may know and believe that the Father is in Me, and I in Him" (John 10:25,38).

The evidence God has given man is extensive, all the words and works of Christ. This is the basis for our belief in Him and it is the basis for our teaching about Him. Spiritual integrity compels us to believe and teach what Christ, who is our very life, believed and taught.

> "All authority has been given to Me in heaven and on earth. Go therefore and make disciples of all the nations, baptizing them in the name of the Father and of the Son and of the Holy Spirit. teaching them to observe all things that I have commanded you; and lo, I am with you always, even to the end of the age. Amen" (Matt. 28:18-20).

References

1. William Hendriksen, *New Testament Commentary Galatians Ephesians* (Grand Rapids: Baker Book House, 1979), pp. 212, 213.

2. W. E. Vine, *An Expository Dictionary of New Testament Words* (Westwood, New Jersey: Fleming H. Revell Company, 1966), p. 243.

3. Everett F. Harrison, *A Short Life of Christ* (Grand Rapids: Wm. B. Eerdmans Publishing Company, 1979), p. 98.

4. Rudolf Bultmann, *Jesus Christ and Mythology* (New York: Charles Scribner's Sons, 1958), pp. 71, 79.

5. G. Campbell Morgan, *Christ And The Bible* (London: Charles Higham And Son Limited, n.d.), pp.14, 15.

6. Francis A. Schaeffer, *The Great Evangelical Disaster* (Westchester, Illinois: Crossway Books, 1984), pp. 57, 61.

7. John A. T. Robinson, *But That I Can't Believe* (London: Collins Fontana Books, 1967), p. 30.

8. Harrison, *op cit*, p. 267.

9. G. Campbell Morgan, *The Teaching of Christ* (London: Hodder and Stoughton, n.d.), p. 39.

10. John Bunyan, *The Holy War* (Grand Rapids: Baker Book House, 1977), p. 142.

11. E. M. Bounds, *Power Through Prayer* (Grand Rapids: Zondervan Publishing House, 1975), p. 13.

12. Alva J. McClain, *The Greatness Of The Kingdom* (Winona Lake, Indiana: BMH Books, 1059), p. 5.

13. C. S. Lewis, *God In The Dock* (Grand Rapids: Eerdmans Publishing Company, 1970), p. 158.

14. *ibid*, p. 160.

15. Shirley MacLaine, *Dancing In The Light* (New York: Bantam Books, 1985), p. 121.

16. Herbert Lockyer, *What Jesus Taught About...* (Eastbourne: Victory Press, 1976), p.46.

17. T. R. Glover, *The Jesus of History* (London: Student Christian Movement, 1918), p.95.

18. John Walvoord, *The Holy Spirit* (Grand Rapids: Zondervan Publishing House, 1954), p. 10.

19. *ibid*, p. 12.

20. William Hendriksen, *New Testament Commentary Gospel Of John* (Edinburgh: The Banner of Truth Trust, 1954), p. 275.

21. Walvoord, *op cit*, p.83.

22. Fredrick Louis Godet, *Commentary On The Gospel Of John* (Grand Rapids: Zondervan Publishing House, 1070), p. 383.

23. B. B. Warfield, *Biblical And Theological Studies* (Philadelphia: The Presbyterian and Reformed Publishing Company, 1968), pp. 217-219.

24. Alan W. Watts, *Beat Zen, Square Zen and Zen* (Harmoundsworth, Middlesex: Penquin Books Limited, 1976), p. 10.

25. John B. Noss and David S. Noss, *Man's Religions*, 7th Edition (New York: Macmillan Publishing Company, 1984), pp. 192,193.

26. Quoted in Bernard Ramm, *A Handbook of Contemporary Theology* (Grand Rapids: Wm. B. Eerdmans Publishing Company, 1966), p. 117.

27. Harper and Row, *The Analytical Greek Lexicon* (New York: Harper and Row, n.d.), p. 336.

28. *ibid*, p. 17.

29. Morgan, *op cit*, p. 135.

30. *Back To Godhead, No. 46, We Belong to Krisna*, p. 7.

I am among you as the One who serves.

Luke 22:27

The Jews expected Messiah to be a prince; but God declared that He should be born a working man.

James Stalker, *Imago Christi*

As the cross is the sign of submission, so the towel is the sign of service.

Richard Foster, *Celebration of Discipline*

I believe with all my heart that in order to speak to this generation we must act like a Bible-believing people. We can emphasize a mess-age faithful to the Bible and the purity of the visible church, but if we do not practice this truth we cannot expect anyone to listen to us.

Francis Schaeffer, *No Little People*

Who among you fears the Lord? Who obeys the voice of His Servant?

Isaiah 50:10

How much are we still governed by our natural likes and dislikes? How far have we been captivated by the spirit of the Crucified?

Howard Guinness, *Sacrifice*

It does not take much of a man to be a disciple, but it takes all of him that there is.

J. Dwight Pentecost, *Design For Discipleship*

6

CHRIST THE SERVANT

What we believe is the basis for what we become. In the preceding chapter we considered Christ's basic beliefs and teaching. His purpose during His days on earth was not simply to teach men certain things, but to transform them into His likeness by the truth He taught. Today, as then, it is impossible to become like Christ apart from believing His teaching. It is not enough just to agree with Him. His truth must be received, believed and applied in our lives. Conviction is demanded and commitment is expected. The challenge Paul gives in Romans 12:2 applies to all Christians, 'Do not be conformed to this world, but be transformed by the renewing of your mind, that you may prove what is that good and acceptable and perfect will of God.'

A renewed mind does not come as the result of agreeing, only from believing! Knowing and doing God's will is the natural outworking of our commitment to Him and His teaching. Believing like Christ is integral to becoming like Him, and becoming like Him involves Christian service. Our good works are important. They will never save us, that is the domain of faith and grace alone (Eph. 2:8,9). We are not saved by works, but by a faith that works, and our works are not the root but the fruit of salvation. When we are 'born again' it is as natural to serve Christ as it is for a living fruit tree to produce fruit.

The Messiah came as a Servant. This surprised and troubled

many people. Isaiah prophesied that when the Christ came He would be called 'Wonderful, Counselor, Mighty God, Everlasting Father, Prince of Peace' and that He would sit on David's throne ruling in justice forever (Isa. 9:6,7). Such a prediction suited Jewish expectations. But when He came as 'a root out of dry ground', having 'no form or comeliness ... no beauty that we should desire Him ... despised and rejected... a man of sorrows and acquainted with grief' they did not receive Him as their promised Sovereign (Isa. 53:2,3). They could not accept this coming as the prelude to the crown, His eternal throne and His rule of earth and heaven. There was no place in their plans for a suffering Servant of Jehovah.

Yet, the same prophet who prophesied the coming King also predicted God's method of exaltation, 'Behold! My Servant whom I uphold ... He shall be extolled and be very high' (Isa. 42:1; 52:13). He would 'be very high' but first He would make Himself of no reputation, take the form of a servant and come in human likeness (Phil. 2:7). This was the unexpected step, stooping to serve, transforming the servant's towel as well as the sceptre into symbols of His rule. The 1st century Jews struggled with this as do many 20th century Christians. To rule in glory and power with Christ is appealing. To serve in humility, to die in rejection as He did, seems appalling. But if we are to walk with Him, the path will certainly lead through service, if not death, on the way to eternal glory in His presence.

Jesus does not call Himself a servant in the Gospels, although they show Him in this capacity constantly. But in them He does give what may be considered His two-fold statement of service: 'For even the Son of Man did not come to be served, but to serve, and to give His life a ransom for many' (Mark 10:45, also Matt. 20:28). Serving God and others characterized His life and giving Himself in obedience to God characterized the end of His life on the cross. Following His example the life of the believer should be a life of service. This is a distinguishing and observable feature of true Christianity. Our service will assume many forms, just as His did, yet it must be offered in the obedience and humility evident in Him.

Areas of Christ's Service

Mark is the action Gospel, short and to the point, presenting Christ as the Perfect Servant. The word 'immediately' and its derivatives are used 41 times, 10 times in the first chapter alone. It is a book that speaks of things getting done! Christ's Servanthood spreads throughout this Gospel, but is revealed in a special way in the events covering about 24 hours recorded in Mark 1:14-35. In this chapter Christ's baptism is dealt with in 3 verses and His temptations in only 2 (Mark 1:9-13).

Then, in verses 14-35 Mark records the events of what we may assume to have been a somewhat typical day of service in Christ's life.

(i) v 14, '*Preaching* the gospel of the kingdom of God.'

(ii) vv 16-20, *Calling* men whom He would train to be His disciples.

(iii) vv 21,22, *Teaching* in the synagogue in an astonishing and authoritative way.

(iv) vv 23-26, *Exorcising* an unclean spirit from a man in the Capernaum synagogue.

(v) vv 29-32, *Healing* physically, first Peter's mother-in-law, and then all those who were brought to Him.

(vi) v 35, *Praying* early the next morning after all the activity of the previous day.

It is interesting that following such a full and intense day of ministry He sought refreshment in the Father's presence through prayer.

Of course there are other areas of service which can be identified in Christ's life. Most notably, perhaps, is that not only did He preach publicly, but He engaged in personal witness and soulwinning. This, along with the areas mentioned by Mark, exemplify His service and show us ways in which we may serve.

The Way Christ Served

As important as the variety of areas of service is the way in which He served. Several aspects are evident throughout His ministry.

(i) The first of these is that He served in the power of the Holy

Spirit. In chapter four we reviewed Christ's temptations. There we noted that He was 'led by the Spirit' into confrontation in the wilderness with the devil and that when this was over He 'returned in the power of the Spirit to Galilee' (Matt. 4:1; Luke 4:14). His return to Galilee marked the beginning of the service carried out during His public ministry, service rendered in the Spirit's power.

This is one of the most important lessons we can learn about Christ as a servant. If we do not understand this we will not be able to emulate in an effective and spiritual way His work. The relationship between the Son and the Spirit was part of the Father's plan. Isaiah spoke pro-phetically of it saying: 'Behold! My Servant whom I uphold, My Elect One in whom My soul delights! I have set My Spirit upon Him' (42:l).

From the beginning, Christ understood this power to be His resource for service. Following His temptations we find Him in Nazareth of Galilee, where, in the synagogue He opens His ministry by quoting from Isaiah: 'The Spirit of the Lord God is upon Me, because the Lord has anointed Me to preach good tidings to the poor ..." (Isa. 61:l-3). Here Christ acknowledges that all His service is to be performed in the power of the Spirit.

If the Son of God served in this way, what hope is there for us who seek to follow Him if we attempt to do so by any other power? We have no power apart from that of Christ given to us through His indwelling Spirit. Anything which seems to be spiritual power other than this is of the flesh. If we are to do the Lord's work in the Lord's way - it will be in the power of the Lord's Spirit. Christ promised this power before His ascension, telling the disciples to wait in Jerusalem until they received it:

'It was to be something previously unknown to them, but suddenly to come upon them from another world. It was to be nothing less than God Himself entering into them with the purpose of ultimately reproducing His own likeness within them.'[1]

The disciples stood at a spiritual point of transition, they waited and received according to Jesus' promise. Since then, in receiving Christ as Saviour we receive also the Spirit who empowers us for service. To our understanding of Ephesians 2:8,9 for the new birth we must add the next verse which declares that 'We are His workmanship, created in Christ Jesus for good works, which God prepared beforehand that we should walk in them' (Eph. 2:10).

It may sound trite but it is a truth overlooked today: 'we are saved to serve'. Service performed in the power of the Holy Spirit is seldom witnessed by us in the Western world. While it is true that there have been times of revival, they have been exceptional times. The rule has not been revival, but resistance of the Spirit, often by the Church, always by the enemy. This has produced a growing resentment on the part of the world against the Church, which in turn, has led to its seeming irrelevance. To counter this trend the temptation has been to turn to new methods, even a new message, one more easily received by secular people. Yielding in this way is denial of the first lesson to be learned from the Servant of Jehovah who served in the anointing of the Holy Spirit. It is not a new method nor a new message that is needed, simply a return to the source of power from which Christ drew during His ministry.

(ii) Christ served in the power of the Spirit and in true humility as well. In Matthew 11:29 we find His invitation, 'Take My yoke upon you and learn from Me, for I am gentle and lowly in heart, and you will find rest for your souls.' This is perhaps as close to a self-description as Christ gives in the Gospels. His invitation is to *learn from Him*; that is what a disciple is, a learner. What we are to learn, in part, is to be like Him in gentleness and lowliness. These are disarming attributes. In our aggressive age how compelling is the calm and unassuming character of true Christianity.

It was this quality which overwhelmed His disciples in the upper room on the night He was betrayed. All 12 gathered there, feet dusty from travel, and no servant to perform the lowly task of washing them clean. The need was present and they all sat through the meal, no one moving to meet it. Then Christ rose, 'laid aside His garments, took a towel and girded Himself. After that, He poured water into a basin and began to wash the disciples' feet, and to wipe them with the towel with which He was girded' (John 13:4,5). When He had finished He said, 'I have given you an example, that you should do as I have done' (John 13:15). In humility Christ performed a literal act which symbolized the wide sphere of Christian service.

Some consider what He did only as a possible third ordinance for the Church and in rebelling against this reject its teaching also. Francis Schaeffer has written, 'It is ten thousand times better to wash each other's feet in a literal way than never to wash anybody's feet in any way'.[2] Many Christians, in refusing this specific act of humble service, seem to refuse any act of humble service.

> 'In some ways we would prefer to hear Jesus' call to deny father and mother, houses and land for the sake of the gospel, than His word to wash feet. Radical self-denial gives us the feel of adventure. But in service we are banished to the mundane, the ordinary, the trivial.'[3]

It is a mark of spiritual maturity to understand that the mundane, when performed by the Spirit's power and in Christ's name, is transformed. It is the little which becomes much because God is in it. It is the cup of cold water given as a disciple for which there is Divine reward (Matt. 10:42).

(iii) A third characteristic of Christ's ministry is that He always served with compassion. It is entirely possible to do a good thing in a bad way. The Pharisees in Jesus' day had an 'unkind way of being *kind*, an unloving way of being *loving*'.[4] They not only performed good deeds for the wrong reason, self-advancement and advertisement, but in the wrong way as well. Their lack of compassion removed the heart from what they did and lost for them any love their service might have generated in themselves or others. By contrast, Christ's service was characterized by compassion. Five times in the Gospels it is recorded that He saw a crowd of people in need and was moved with compassion for them (Matt. 9:36; 14:14; 15:32; Mark 6:34; 8:2). And an additional three times, as He was performing a physical miracle, both the miracle and His compassion are emphasized (Matt. 20:34; Mark 1:41; Luke 7:13).[5]

Another basic lesson we must learn from Christ the servant is to *see* our world as He does. Compassion is a way of seeing. One of the New Testament words translated 'compassion' is *splanchnizomai*, which means 'to be moved as to ones inwards'.[6] It relates to 'those inner parts of man which are the seat of the deepest emotions ... It denotes a gut reaction, an intense visceral emotion, the deep feelings of man for man which clutch at the stomach, it also suggests strong anger at the situation which has reduced the man to his present circumstances'.[7]

Christ beheld the unbelief which held men captive and 'was moved with compassion for them' (Matt. 9:36). He saw the sickness which invaded the human form because of the fall, and was 'moved with compassion' (Mark 1:41). He was morally and spiritually outraged at these unnatural conditions arising from sin and had compassion on the sinner. He did all in compassion, beginning with the greatest act ever of compassion, His incarnation by which He literally came along side of humanity in serving and sacrificial love.

Two Qualities of a Good Servant

There are two qualities inherent in a good servant and perfectly applied in Christ's life. By these the power of the Spirit, humility and compassion may be focused upon a task.

The first quality is that a servant *must see the need*. This Christ did from a hill overlooking Jerusalem. He saw the multitudes and 'was moved with compassion for them, because they were weary and scattered, like sheep having no shepherd' (Matt. 9:36). The eye of compassion beheld the need. Yet, had He stopped there the need would have remained.

A second step is required. *A good servant must give himself to meet the need*. This Christ did from another hill also overlooking Jerusalem where 'He humbled Himself and became obedient to the point of death, even the death of the cross' (Phil. 2:8). It was only after seeing the need and giving Himself to meet the need that He could say, 'It is finished' (John 19:30)! In the key verse of Mark's Gospel Christ has given us the two divisions of His ministry: to *serve* and to *give His life* (Mark 10:45). Both culminated on Calvary and are clearly visible for the world to see and the Christian to follow.

Christ's example is our pattern for service. It is never enough just to acknowledge the need which exists, never enough simply to yearn for the lost and brokenness of our world. The second step of commitment is required. We must give ourselves to God so that through us He may meet the need. The Commission Christ gives to His Church is expressed this way in John's Gospel: 'As the Father has sent Me, I also send you' (John 20:21). We are sent by Him to do what He did in the way He did it. We are to see as He saw and give ourselves to meet the need revealed by the eye of compassion.

Christ's most frequently repeated command in Scripture is not 'receive Me', but 'follow Me'. It seems there are many who receive but fewer who follow. So long as we are selective in our service we will not be very effective. If we are willing to emulate only those aspects of Christ's service which suit us we will never really serve Him. All service is not of equal value in the eyes of the Lord! There will be a time when some will say to Him, 'Lord, Lord, have we not prophesied in Your name, cast out demons in Your name, and done many wonders in Your name?' And in that day He will say to them, 'I never knew you; depart from Me' (Matt. 7:22,23). All that is done 'in Jesus' name' does not please Him nor conform to His pattern for serving. All who serve Him have not received Him. All who have received Him do not serve Him acceptably.

There are many types of service, but for our study we will focus on two.

Self-serving Service

It is possible to seem to serve Christ and others, when we are only serving ourselves. What sometimes passes for self-sacrificial service may be pathological - our own need to be needed. Our service may be the means to ends other than the Lord's glory or meeting the need of another. Self-serving service bears certain distinguishing marks.

(i) Those serving in this way generally have a constant need to be noticed. The greater the degree of visibility, the stronger the motivation to serve.

(ii) What appeals to them is usually the 'bigger and better' acts of service, tasks worthy of their time and talents.

(iii) They are prone to render service for results. Souls may become statistics, good deeds simply notches for the 'gospel gun' and what is done for another obligates them to return the same.

(iv) Self-serving service is often short-sighted. In serving to the end, the end is reinterpreted. So long as it is convenient and not too costly it may be given.

Christ-like Service

By contrast we are given in the Gospels the example of Christ-like service. Enabled by the Spirit of God we may follow in the footsteps of Christ, held faithful to the end regardless of the cost. Such service also bears certain distinguishing marks.

(i) Christ-like service is characterized by hiddenness. Knowing that God knows is enough! Often Christ told those whom He helped to tell no one. In the Sermon on the Mount He taught that our 'charitable deeds' are not to be done 'before men to be seen by them'. There are to be no trumpets, we are not to play to the crowd (Matt. 6:1,2). He also urged prayer in 'the secret place', noticed by God and openly rewarded by Him. Street-corner praying to be seen by others is to be avoided (Matt. 6:5,6). In contemplating Isaiah's Servant of Jehovah, F. B. Meyer has written, 'The only work that God approves, that is permanent and fruitful, that partakes of the nature of Christ, is that which neither seeks nor needs advertisement'.[8] When we serve as Christ did we desire God's approval but do not require man's.

(ii) In true Christian service cups of cold water given to little ones count a great deal with God (Matt. 10:42). He does not measure our service by its public dimension. The Christ-like servant 'finds it almost impossible to distinguish the small from the large service'.[9] Jesus spoke to Nicodemus and the Samaritan Woman as well as to the thousands on many hillsides. He took little ones onto His lap and touched lepers with His hands. He taught that faithfulness over a few things is the way to rule over many (Matt. 25:21, 23). In the Old Testament Zechariah warned against despising 'the day of small things' (Zech. 4:10). In the New Testament Christ didn't. He didn't and we shouldn't regardless of the world's example and pressures.

(iii) Results are important. The Christ-like servant knows this but also knows that they aren't everything. The first result desired should be service given that honours the Lord and is acceptable to Him. If this is first all that follows will be clarified by it. 'True service is free of the need of calculating results. It delights only in service.'[10] The means as well as the ends matter in serving God.

(iv) Faithfulness is the foundation of Christ-like service. Many receive the Lord who do not follow Him throughout life. The unwritten history of the Church is filled with those who put a hand to the plough only to release it before the furrow was finished. In considering Christ's example it is fitting that His first recorded words were, 'I must be about My Father's business' (Luke 2:49). And that among His final words were these, 'It is finished' (John 19:30). It is imperative that we meditate on His faithfulness and His call to follow Him. Follow Him! How long? Where? What does He expect along the way? What does His example say in response to such questions?

The great English maritime hero Sir Francis Drake once prayed, 'Oh Lord God, when Thou givest to us Thy servants to endeavour any great matter, teach us also to know that it is not the beginning but the continuing of the same until it be thoroughly finished which yieldeth the true glory; through Him who for the finishing of Thy work laid down His life, our Redeemer, Jesus Christ, Amen'.[11]

A thing thoroughly finished, that is Christ' example. And that is His expectation. Christ-like service involves faithfulness in doing His will and not our own and faithfulness in finishing the race. The critical factor in our life of service is not how far we have come, but the distance remaining. Sometimes the last lap is the hardest. The end brought Christ to Calvary and the cry of the crowd to come down from the cross and save Himself. But He didn't (Luke 23:35).

The True Disciple

As not all service is of equal value to the Lord, so also are all disciples not the same. Jesus said, 'If anyone serves Me, let him follow Me' (John 12:26). Serving Christ involves following Him. The word often used in the New Testament for disciple is *mathetes*, which means 'a learner ... (one who) imitates his teacher'.[12] A true disciple of Christ is one who is learning from Him and following Him. A degree of discernment is required for us to understand the New Testament's teaching on discipleship. In reading the Gospels we discover three ways the word disciple is used.

(i) The first way simply indicates a person who is curious about Christ. Generally such interest is sparked by a miracle or some new idea expressed in His teaching.

(ii) The second use of the word describes those who have followed their curiosity on to accept as true what Christ taught. They recognize in His words a higher than human wisdom. Yet, as in John 12:42, such 'disciples' may believe but fail to confess Christ, considering the cost to be too great.

(iii) The final use of the word relates to those who are 'true disciples'. They not only believe but confess and are willing to fully commit themselves to the One who has taught them.[13] Christ-like service is rendered by true disciples. It demands a high degree of commitment, is distinguished by faithfulness and characterized by obedience. It is obedience which separates the curious from the committed! 'While one is in the place of disobedience he is not in the place of discipleship, for the Bible demands absolute obedience to the Word of God and the authority of Jesus Christ as a necessary prerequisite to discipleship.'[14]

Eric Liddell, a gold medallist of the 1924 Olympic Games, wrote only one book before his death in a prison camp in China. In it he says, 'Obedience to God's will is the secret of spiritual knowledge and insight. It is not willingness to know, but willingness to *do* (obey) God's will that brings enlightenment and certainty regarding spiritual truth'.[15] The curious are willing to know; the committed are willing to do. Doing confirms our faith to ourselves and affirms it to the watching world.

It is a human trait to follow. We all follow another individual, an ideology, someone or something. Equally we all serve. It may be self or another, but it is certain that we serve someone or something. No one succeeds in serving nothing! To follow Jesus Christ, to be His disciple, is to walk in truth and light. It is to live a life of service that imitates and honours Him, bringing praise to Him and peace to ourselves.

> The ministry of Jesus was... the revelation of the life that God had ever been living in the blue depths of heaven; and if once we can learn the principles of that life which filled hundreds and thousands of homes with blessing and joy during those marvellous years of earthly ministry, we shall have a model on which to form our own service to God and man. Our Lord's life and ministry revealed the ideal of service.'[16]

'I heard a call,
"Come follow",
That was all.

Earth's joys grew dim,
My soul went after Him,
I rose and followed -
That was all.

Will you not follow
If you hear Him call?

References

1. A. W. Tozer, *The Divine Conquest* (London: Oliphants, 1970, p. 87.

2. Francis A. Schaeffer, *No Little People* (Downers Grove, Illinois: InterVarsity Press, 1974), p. 68.

3. Richard Foster, *Celebration of Discipline* (London: Hodder and Stoughton, 1980), p.110.

4. James Stalker, *The Life and Teaching of Jesus Christ* (Edinburgh: The Church of Scotland Committee on the Religious Instruction of Youth, 1965), p. 125.

5. Harold K. Moulton, *The Challenge Of The Concordance* (London: Samuel Bagster and Sons Ltd, 1977), p. 259.

6. W. E. Vine, *An Expository Dictionary of New Testament Words* (Westwood, New Jersey: Fleming H. Revell Company, 1966), p. 218.

7. Os Guinness, *The Dust of Death* (Downers Grove, Illinois: InterVarsity Press, 1973), pp. 383, 384.

8. F. B. Meyer, *Christ In Isaiah* (Grand Rapids: Zondervan Publishing House, 1957), p. 35.

9. Foster, *op cit*, p. 112.

10. *Ibid*.

11. Quoted in *Child-Life Newsletter No. 6*, English L'Abri, December, 1983.

12. Vine, *op cit*, p. 316.

13. J. Dwight Pentecost, *Design for Discipleship* (Grand Rapids: Zondervan Publishing House, 1971), p. 40.

14. *Ibid*.

15. Eric Liddell, *The Disciplines of the Christian Life* (London: Triangle/SPCK, 1985), p. 27.

16. Meyer, *op cit*, p. 3

We have lost the eternal youthfulness of Christianity and aged into calculating manhood. We seldom pray in earnest for the extraordinary, the limitless, the glorious.

Unknown

If prayer is anything at all, it is a thing to be done.

George MacDonald

The realization of fellowship with God will never be more than a theory save as prayer becomes a practice.

G. Campbell Morgan

Prayer... is... a state rather than an act. A holy prayer is the Spirit of God speaking through the infirmities of a human soul - God's breath in man, returning to his birth.

Austin Phelps, *The Still Hour*

I love the Lord, because He has heard My voice and my supplications. Because He has inclined His ear to me. Therefore I will call upon Him as long as I live.

Psalm 116:1,2

Through prayer we become co-workers with the Lord God Almighty. We move from time into eternity, sharing in the eternal counsels of God.

P. Johnstone, *Operation World*

7

CHRIST-LIKE PRAYING

Prayer is communication. It is becoming acquainted with God by spending time in His presence; being with Him and knowing that He is there with us. The time spent may be passed in speaking as well as listening, for both are essential elements in true communication.

Christ spoke often about prayer and practised it continually. What He said and did form the foundation for the practice of prayer by His followers. The Bible is filled with examples of men and women who made petition for themselves, intercession for others and offered praise, adoration and thanksgiving to God. All they teach us about prayer is important. Yet what Christ describes in His teaching and demonstrates in His practice of prayer is of special value by virtue of the fact of who He is. His words on prayer are those God chose to say as man to men about communion between man and God. His prayers are those the Son of God prayed to His Father. If we fail to follow His instruction and example we deny ourselves the power of true prayer and the joy of true communion.

As the 20th century closes there is a great need for praying Christians, those who understand that through prayer God is able not only to change them, but history as well. This He can do with no violence to our free will nor violation of His sovereignty. That He can do so is both the fact and mystery of prayer.

Within the widening context of current religion quite a lot is being said about prayer. Although it is not denied, often it is redefined and thus reduced to the level of dialogue or meditation. As the East continues to influence the West, as exemplified in the New Age Movement, people are urged to visualize the transmission of light and the sending of 'thought forms of love' to dispel the world's darkness.[1] Thus prayer becomes 'The Great Invocation', but there is no clarity regarding the God or gods being invoked.[2]

It may well be that the true religion of the 20th century western world is materialism. A frightening feature of which is that it freely allows the retention of a remnant of Judeo-Christian belief to soothe our spiritual conscience. Yet as we become increasingly a Post-Christian culture even this Christian memory is in decline; and our direction seems to be toward the merging of materialism and humanism, a union which, in its end, may fully erode the practice of prayer. In humanism's founding document, the *Humanist Manifesto I*, affirmation nine states, 'In place of the old attitudes involved in worship and prayer the humanist finds his religious emotions expressed in a heightened sense of personal life and in a cooperative effort to promote social well being'.[3]

In this refocusing, prayer to God is replaced by an emphasis upon self and society. These are both subjects of great need but can never be the source of power to effect change in line with God's will, that power rests in Him alone and is accessible to us through prayer.

For Christians not to pray when confronted by such powerful and ungodly movements is to seek to stand against them on their human level. Then it becomes the confrontation of ideology against ideology, rather than of Divinely-empowered truth against man's error. To speak the truth less than prayerfully is to lessen its impact upon society.

For the Christian, prayerlessness is a sin, and prayerless-praying is no less a sin. If we pray from habit and not from commitment and conviction, then ours is prayerless-praying. Such 'speaking of words only' will make little difference to men and will not further the cause of Christ among them. Dr. Martyn Lloyd-Jones has written, 'Prayer is beyond any question the highest activity of the human soul. Man is at his greatest and highest when, upon his knees, he comes face to face with God'.[4] This is where the power rests. It is from such face to face encounters with God that we may turn to face the world, assured that His power flows through us and that even our heedless generation may be halted before destruction.

While churchmen and theologians debate the validity of prayer Christ never did. He no more attempted to prove its value than He tried to prove the existence of the Father. For Him prayer is simply the assumed activity of the Christian. It is as natural to spiritual life as breathing is to physical life - and as essential. Ultimately it is He Himself who is 'the supreme argument for prayer'.[5] Because Christ prayed we are compelled to pray, and in the pattern of His praying the power of God is placed at our disposal; defined and directed by His will. The disciples said to the Lord, 'Teach us to pray' (Luke 11:1). This He did, in word and deed.

The following two sections deal with Christ's teaching on prayer and His own practice of it. In the references considered we have His personal prayer manifesto.

Christ's Teaching on Prayer

As Christ moved among men He taught many things. Central to His teaching is what He said about prayer, it is the breath which animates the body of all His doctrine. He taught that to pray is to hold a high view of God; it is to acknowledge that HE IS, that He is holy and that men must come before Him in humility. He stressed that prayer is spiritual rather than formal; the communication of our spirit with God who is Spirit. He also characterized prayer as the spontaneous outpouring of the human heart, free flowing communication between creature and Creator.

In the Gospels we are given a record of what Christ taught about praying. If we are going to pray as He did we must understand and apply the biblical principles revealed through the following passages. First we will consider His teaching. In each instance the reference is given for personal study along with a brief statement summarizing what He taught. After this, several lessons are listed which suggest some of His main points of emphasis.

Matthew 5:44; Luke 6:28. Teaching: 'Pray for those who spitefully use you and persecute you.'

Matthew 6:5-15; Luke 11:2-4. Teaching: The 'Learner's' or 'Model Prayer'. This prayer is sometimes called 'The Lord's Prayer'. The following outline may be helpful.

> v9a, *Invocation*, 'Our Father in heaven'
>
> vv9b,10 *Petitions Relating to God:* (i) 'Hallowed be Your name'; (ii) 'Your kingdom come'; (iii) 'Your will be done'.
>
> vv11-13a *Petitions Relating to Man:* (i) 'Give us this day our daily bread'; (ii) 'Forgive us our debts, As we forgive our debtors'; (iii) 'Do not lead us into temptation, But deliver us from the evil one'.
>
> v13b *Benediction,* 'For Yours is the kingdom and the power and the glory forever. Amen'.

Matthew 7:7-11; Luke 11:5-13: In a prayer-parable Christ teaches that we are to persist in praying: ask, knock, seek. (cf Luke 18:1-8)

Matthew 9:37-39: Surveying the lost and needy of Jerusalem Christ urges prayer that labourers will enter God's harvest.

Matthew 18:19,20 Christ teaches the spiritual benefit and power in prayer present when we are united and gathered in His name.

Matthew 18:21-35; Mark 11:25,26 In another prayer-parable Christ teaches the necessity of forgiving others if our prayers are to be answered. (cf Matt. 6:12)

Matthew. 21:13; Mark 11:17; Luke 19:46: Each of the Synoptics contain Christ's teaching that His 'house shall be called a house of prayer'. Mark adds that prayer is to be made there 'for all nations'.

Matthew 21:18-22; Mark 11:20-24: In the context of the cursed fig tree Christ emphasizes that faith is essential to effective prayer.

Matthew 23:14; Mark 12:40; Luke 20:47: Here Christ teaches that not all prayer is true prayer, nor are all who seem to pray true Christians. He calls the scribes and Pharisees hypocrites and their praying only pretence which brings greater condemnation upon themselves.

Matthew 24:20; Mark 13:18: In the Discourse on the Mount of Olives, Christ speaks of prayer for deliverance during the future Great Tribulation.

Mark 9:14-20: Christ explains the value of combined prayer and fasting to the disciples indicating that this is the power by which a certain boy is delivered from demon possession.

Mark 13:33; Luke 21:36: In the context of Christ's promised future return He urges His followers to 'watch and pray'.

Luke 18:1-8: Christ teaches the importance of perseverance in prayer. This time He uses the illustration of the widow who would not be denied. (cf Matt. 7:7,11; Luke 11:5-13)

Luke 18:9-14: He follows the above parable with another in which He teaches the right and wrong way to pray as illustrated by the proud Pharisee and humble tax collector.

John 14:12-14; 15:16; 16:23-26: In these verses Christ teaches that answered prayer is linked with faith and is offered in His name.

John 15:7: Here we learn that in addition to faith and praying in Christ's name, His Word also has a part in effective prayer. In the context of the Vine and Branch teaching He associates answered prayer with abiding in Him and His Word abiding in us.

Lessons from Christ's Teaching on Prayer

(i) Christ gives us a model (Matthew 6:5-15) to guide us in forming our own prayers. The prayer He taught the disciples is not a substitute for personal prayers, rather a pattern for their development. Prayer which conforms to the 'Learner's Prayer' contains the elements essential to effective praying. D. Martyn Lloyd-Jones observes, 'I have always been comforted by this thought, that whatever I may forget in my own private prayers, as long as I pray the Lord's Prayer I have at any rate covered all the principles. On condition, of course, that I am not merely mechanically repeating the words, but am really praying from my heart and with my mind and with my whole being'.[6] The order given in this prayer is important. It begins with God, then moves to man. This is a good pattern for us to apply in our prayers.

(ii) *Faith* is an essential to true prayer. It is not the length of our prayers but the strength of our faith that makes the difference. The reason much of our praying seems ineffectual is simply because we do not believe it works. At heart we may doubt that God hears, is willing or able to answer. While doubt of itself is not a sin, to allow it to persist is. We must confront our doubt before the Lord and ask Him to help us overcome it and as doubt declines faith increases.

To pray as Christ we must pray in faith. In his classic on prayer, *The Still Hour*, Austin Phelps writes,

153

'An intrepid faith in prayer will always give it unction ... I come to my devotions this morning, on an errand of real life. This is no romance and no farce. I do not come here to go through a form of words. I have no hopeless desires to express. I have an object to gain. I have an end to accomplish. This is a *business* in which I am about to engage. An astronomer does not turn his telescope to the skies with a more reasonable hope of penetrating those distant heavens, than I have of reaching the mind of God, by lifting up my heart at the throne of grace. This is the privilege of my calling of God in Christ Jesus. Even my faltering voice is now to be heard in heaven, and it is to put forth a power there, the results of which only God can know, and only eternity can develop.'⁷

(iii) *Perseverance* is important in prayer. Christ teaches this especially in His prayer-parables. From these we learn that we are not only to ask, but to knock and seek as well. In our age of instant almost everything, we may, presumptuously, expect instant answers to prayer. If they do not come we may become annoyed with God and stop making our requests, and if we do this we forfeit not only the object of the prayer but the spiritual growth which may be God's purpose in what we interpret as delay or refusal.

Behind our failure to persist in prayer is often the fact that we do not really expect an answer. For us it may be the *act* of praying and not its *end* that becomes important. Prayer can become simply something we do rather than the means of getting something done. Prayer is not an act to eliminate our guilt - I am supposed to pray, so I pray, and that takes care of that! True prayer accomplishes things and if we have a soul-belief that this is true, that in prayer we enter into the work of God among men on earth, that we become co-labourers with Him, then we will persist.

(iv) *Relationships* are important in prayer. We would expect our relationship with God to be important. But there is not only the vertical, our relationship with Him, but the horizontal, our relationship with others, as well. Both affect our effectiveness in prayer. It is no good coming to the Father for forgiveness, or for anything, if we will not forgive our fellow man. Forgiveness is a heart attitude and a hard heart toward others is not the source of vibrant praying. Prayer is more than a matter between man and God, it is also a matter of the relationship between man and man.

(v) *God's House* is to be a place of prayer. In this final lesson we face a spiritual truth seldom applied to day. Can we call the place where we worship a 'house of prayer'? Christ teaches that we are to have our personal private place for prayer. But just as clearly He tells us of the great power arising from united prayer offered by those assembled in His name. He does not identify His Father's house as a place of preaching or serving, but He does call it a 'house of prayer'. It is important that we know this and consider our conduct in God's house. When we gather there, is prayer given high priority? Or do we consider it an intrusion into our pro-gramme of music and ministry, necessary perhaps, but an intrusion none-the-less. I have often wondered how many join in the prayer being worded by someone in their midst. How many are praying? How many are waiting till the 'amen' to go on to the next thing? I wonder, did Christ's mind ever wander as others prayed in His presence?

It is fine for God's house to be used for many things other than prayer. But it is to be known as a place of prayer, where eternal business is transacted which touches not only heaven but all nations under heaven. Christ expressed His anger at those who made an unholy transformation of His Father's house in His day. Can we expect His anger to be any less against us if we do the same today?

Christ's Prayers

The section which follows presents Christ's personal practice of prayer as recorded in the Gospels. In the 24 references considered, 16 times we are told that Christ prayed but His prayer is not given. But though His words are not recorded we often learn the subject of His prayer by considering the context. In the remaining 8 references we are given His prayers, ranging in length from a few words to the entirety of John chapter 17. As we examine each of these 24 accounts the prayer, subject and context are charted. They are listed gospel by gospel and thus not in chronological order.

(i) Matthew 11:25,26; Luke 10:21

The Prayer: "I thank You, Father, Lord of heaven and earth, because You have hidden these things from the wise and prudent and have revealed them to babes. Even so, Father, for so it seemed good in Your sight" (Matt. 11:25,26).

The Subject: Thanksgiving and rejoicing because the Father reveals spiritual truth to the 'simple', those who humbly acknowledge their helplessness and recognize their need of His help.

The Context: This prayer precedes Christ's invitation that we come to Him, take up His yoke and learn from Him.

(ii) Matthew 14:19; Mark 6:41; Luke 9:16; John 6:11

The Prayer: Not recorded

The Subject: A prayer of thanksgiving for the loaves and fish.

The Context: The feeding of the 5,000 at a late hour, in a deserted place.

(iii) Matthew 14:23; Mark 6:46,47; Luke 9:18

The Prayer: Not recorded

The Subject: not recorded

The Context: Christ prays alone on a mountain after the feeding of the 5,000.

(iv) Matthew 15:36; Mark 8:6,7

The Prayer: Not recorded

The Subject: A prayer of thanksgiving for the loaves and fish.

The Context: The feeding of the 4,000; those who had remained with Him three days and had nothing to eat.

(v) Matthew 19:13-15; Mark 10:16

The Prayer: Not recorded

The Subject: Christ blesses little children brought to Him.

The Context: He does this immediately following His teaching on divorce.

(vi) Matthew 26:26-30; Luke 22:17-19

The Prayer: Not recorded

The Subject: Christ blesses the bread and wine as He institutes the Lord's Supper.

The Context: The final night of Christ's life on earth. He spends His last hours with the disciples, teaching them and preparing them for His death.

(vii) Matthew 26:36-46; Mark 14:32, 36-39; Luke 22: 39-46
The Prayer: 'O My Father, if it is possible, let this cup pass from Me; nevertheless, not as I will, but as You will.... O My Father, if this cup cannot pass away from Me unless I drink it, Your will be done' (Matt. 26:39,42).
The Subject: Christ prays for deliverance from the 'cup' of suffering which is before Him at that moment. The 'cup' is not His death. He knows that it must take place and has taught its certainty from the beginning of His ministry. Rather, it is the intense suffering of the moment at hand in Gethsemane, suffering 'whose bitterness and horrors He was then tasting'.[8]
The Context: The Garden of Gethsemane; only hours before Golgotha and His final suffering and death.

(viii) Matthew 27:46; Mark 15:34
The Prayer: 'My God, My God, why have You forsaken Me' (Matt. 27:46)?
The Subject: Christ prays from the cross where He is being 'made sin' for us and is being 'wounded for our transgressions and bruised for our iniquities' (2 Cor. 5:21; Isa. 53:5).
The Context: The fourth of His seven sayings from the Cross. Among the final words He says are these in the form of prayer.

(ix) Mark 1:35
The Prayer: Not recorded
The Subject: Not recorded
The Context: Following a day filled with activity as outlined in Mark 1:14-34, Christ goes to a solitary place to pray a long while before daylight. It is significant that He found refreshment in His Father's presence.

(x) Mark 7:31-37
The Prayer: Not recorded
The Subject: Christ is healing a deaf man who also has an impediment in his speech. 'Then looking up to heaven, He sighed, and said to him, Ephphatha, that is, Be opened' (Mark 7:34). This seems definitely to have been a prayer. His heavenward look indicates that He is including the

Father in what He is about to do and relying upon His power for the miracle. From the Father He turns to the man and, in speaking to him, the healing power is applied. This unusual incident helps us understand that prayer need not always be expressed in words but may take the form of deeds as well. As we live after the pattern of Christ our lives become, in effect, a prayer.

The Context: A miracle of physical healing.

(xi) Luke 3:21
The Prayer: Not recorded
The Subject: Not recorded
The Context: At the moment of His transition from private to public life, marked by His baptism, Christ prayed and 'the heaven was opened'.

(xii) Luke 5:16
The Prayer: Not recorded
The Subject: Not recorded
The Context: After he had healed a leper a great multitude of people gathered around Him to hear Him and be healed by Him. When He completed this ministry, as He often did, 'He ... withdrew into the wilderness to pray'.

(xiii) Luke 6:12,13
The Prayer: Not recorded
The Subject: Not recorded but implied in the context
The Context: 'He went out to the mountain to pray, and continued all night in prayer to God. And when it was day, He called His disciples to Him; and from them He chose twelve whom He also named apostles.' It seems that His night of prayer was for guidance from the Father in choosing these men upon whom would rest the responsibility of establishing the New Testament Church.

(xiv) Luke 9:28,29
The Prayer: Not recorded
The Subject: Not recorded
The Context: The Transfiguration

(xv) Luke 11:1
The Prayer: Not recorded

The Subject: Not recorded

The Context: 'And it came to pass, as He was praying in a certain place, when He ceased, that one of His disciples said to Him, Lord, teach us to pray, as John also taught his disciples.' In response to this request Christ taught His followers the 'Learner's Prayer'. No doubt this request came because the disciples had often watched Christ praying and knew what an important place it had in His life. Their desire to be like Him included their desire to learn to pray as He did.

(xvi) Luke 22:31,32

The Prayer: Not recorded

The Subject: This is an example of Christ's intercession. He prays that as Peter is tempted by Satan, his faith will not fail.

The Context: Christ predicts Peter's denial. In spite of his firm protest Peter fulfils the prediction, finding the temptation of Satan severe. Yet, in the end, his faith is not destroyed.

(xvii) Luke 23:34

The Prayer: 'Father, forgive them, for they do not know what they do.'

The Subject: Christ prays that the Father will forgive those who are crucifying Him.

The Context: The first of His seven sayings from the cross.

(xviii) Luke 23:46

The Prayer: 'Father, into Your hands I commend My spirit.''

The Subject: Our Lord yields Himself to death in our place and commends His spirit, when separated from His body by death, into the Father's hands.

The Context: The last of His seven sayings from the cross. The importance of prayer in His life is emphasized by the fact that He both began and ended His public ministry in prayer. As He prayed at His baptism the heavens opened and now He prays as He prepares to return to heaven.

(xix) Luke 24:30

The Prayer: Not recorded

The Subject: 'As He sat at the table with them, ... He took bread, blessed and broke it, and gave it to them.'

The Context: During one of His post-resurrection appearances He shares a meal with Cleopas and another disciple near Emmaus.

(xx) Luke 24:51
The Prayer: Not recorded
The Subject: Christ blesses His disciples.
The Context: He makes this blessing just before He ascends into heaven.

(xxi) John 11:41,42
The Prayer: "Father, I thank You that You have heard Me. And I know that You always hear Me, but because of the people who are standing by I said this, that they may believe that You sent Me.'
The Subject: Christ's thanksgiving for the assurance that the Father always hears His prayers.
The Context: He speaks to God in prayer and then calls Lazarus forth from the dead to resurrected life.

(xxii) John 12:27,28
The Prayer: "Now My soul is troubled, and what shall I say? Father, glorify Your name."
The Subject: The 'hour' Christ refers to in this prayer is His death. The request that the Father 'save' Him from this is not a plea to escape His earthly purpose, rather a request for His resurrection. By His death and resurrection He brings 'glory' to the Father's name.
The Context: He has just spoken of the grain of wheat which must fall into the ground and die if it is to bring forth fruit. In this context He predicts His death as the means of securing fruit for the Father. It is in this way that He draws men to Himself for salvation.

(xxiii) John 14:16-18
The Prayer: Not recorded
The Subject: Christ tells the disciples that He will pray for the Father to send the Holy Spirit whom He calls 'another Helper' and the 'Spirit of truth'.
The Context: This is part of our Lord's final instruction given to the disciples on the night before His death.

(xxiv) John 17:1-26
The Prayer: This entire chapter contains Christ's prayer which is called

'The Master's Prayer', or sometimes 'The Lord's Prayer'. In the sixteenth century the Reformer Philip Melanchthon said, 'Nothing more dignified, nothing more holy, nothing more fruitful, nothing more pathetic has ever been heard in heaven or earth than this prayer of the very Son of God'.[9]

The Subject: The following outline of 'The Master's Prayer' reveals its three-part emphasis.

vv 1-5, *Personal;* Christ prays for Himself

vv 6-19, *Particular;* Christ prays for His Disciples

    vv 6-12, That they will be secure

    vv 13-19, That they will become sanctified

vv 20-26, *General;* Christ prays for the whole Church.[10]

The Context: Christ offers this prayer after His final instructions are given to His disciples as recorded in John 13-16. The place is somewhere between the upper room in Jerusalem and the Garden of Gethsemane. The last thing He does with the disciples as a group is pray before them and for them.

Lessons From Christ's Prayers

In our Lord's prayers there are lessons which every Christian should learn and apply. The more we pray as Christ did the more like Him we will become in every aspect of life. In 'The Learner's Prayer' Christ taught the disciples, He provides a pattern for prayer, and in His recorded prayers we find this pattern amplified and applied. Among the lessons His prayers provide are these.

(i) *Faith* is the foundation of effective prayers. In His teaching on prayer Christ said, '...Whoever says to this mountain, Be removed and be cast into the sea, and does not doubt in his heart, but believes that those things he says will come to pass, he will have whatever he says. Therefore I say to you, whatever things you ask when you pray, believe that you receive them, and you will have them' (Mark 11:23,24). In His practice of prayer Christ prayed, 'Father, I thank You that You have heard Me. And I know that You always hear Me' (John 11:41,42).

Our Lord had complete faith, being fully assured that the Father always heard all of His prayers. One aspect of our growing likeness to Christ is a similar assurance in our praying. It is entirely natural that we should develop such confidence as its certainty is based upon the answer Christ received to one of His prayers. In John 14:16,17, He told the disciples that He would 'pray the Father, and He will give you another Helper, that He may abide with you forever, even the Spirit of truth whom the world cannot receive, because it neither sees Him nor knows Him for He dwells with you and will be in you'. Christ's answer to this prayer came in the coming of the Holy Spirit who indwells every believer from the instant of their conversion onward. The blessings of this truth are incomparable. And one of its most practical applications is realized in our practice of prayer.

Part of the mystery we attach to prayer is based upon our uncertainty regarding God's will. We reason, 'If only I *knew* God's will I could pray in real faith'. While an element of His purpose will always remain unknown to us, a great deal is known and can be known - probably far more than we realize. Our knowledge of God's will comes to us in two ways: (i) internally, through the indwelling Holy Spirit, (ii) and externally, through the Word of God. It is through the Word that we learn of Christ, observe His life and consider His own prayers. G. Campbell Morgan has written that 'The indwelling Spirit knows the will of God and interprets it to the soul in whom He abides. This He does by unveiling Christ, who is the revelation of the will of God'.[11]

As we acknowledge the Spirit's presence in our lives and yield to Him we are in turn guided by Him in our praying. And as we experience His guidance we in turn pray according to God's will for it is part of the Spirit's ministry to lead us from the known into the unknown regarding God's will. The Holy Spirit, our aid in prayer, comes in answer to Christ's prayer and He teaches us to pray progressively in the will of God, after the pattern of Christ.

Externally, Christ's life recorded in the Gospels helps us to pray in God's will. He came to do the Father's will and as our lives conform to His, they also conform to God's will. It is at this point in particular that Christ's recorded prayers are helpful in shaping our own. We may make the same requests and offer similar praise to God with complete certainty that we do so in His will.

From Christ's prayers we learn that we may pray in complete faith for the following things. (i) John 17:20, the salvation of others; (ii) John 17:9,15,17, the security and sanctification of all who follow Him; (iii) Matthew 9:37,38, labourers to enter God's harvest fields; (iv) Luke 6:12,13, guidance when faced with choices and decisions; (v) Luke 23:34, that those who commit sin will be forgiven; (vi) Luke 22:31,32, that our faith will be strong in temptation. Christ's prayers not only provide a pattern for our own, but they reveal many aspects of God's will as well. Conformity to Christ in prayer enables us to pray believing and in a day in which not many mountains seem to be moved by prayer this is a lesson we must apply.

(ii) Prayer takes *time.* Effective praying cannot be done in a rush. Christ chided the Pharisees for their long prayers only because they were a pretence and not because He opposed long prayers. At times He prayed through the night Himself.

Because true prayer is based upon true faith, there is a link between the degree of faith and the amount of time devoted to praying. If our faith in the value of prayer is small the time we spend praying will be short. We will not spend much time doing something we do not believe in or about which we are uncertain. In *Power Through Prayer*, E. M. Bounds writes,

> 'We would not have any think that the value of their prayer is to be measured by the clock, but our purpose is to impress on our minds the necessity of being much alone with God; and that if this feature has not been produced by our faith, then our faith is of a feeble and surface type. Men who have most fully illustrated Christ in their character, and have most powerfully affected the world for Him, have been men who spent so much time with God as to make it a notable feature of their lives.'[12]

Many of the prayers recorded in the Bible are short, as some of Christ's are. Yet their brevity does not decrease their effectiveness. All prayers do not have to be long but short prayers must be based upon a foundation established through prolonged praying.

'It requires a serious mind and determined heart to pray past the ordinary into the unusual. Most Christians never do.'[13] Perhaps most never do because of the time involved. We are in an eternal rush, caught up in the motion-madness of our age. Baron von Hugel observed that 'Nothing was ever accomplished in a stampede'.[14] This is true of most things in life and is certainly true of prayer.

Take time to be holy, the world rushes on;
Spend much time in secret with Jesus alone -
By looking to Jesus, like Him thou shalt be;
Thy friends in thy conduct His likeness shall see.[15]

Just as holiness requires time, prayer, which is its vital breath, involves time as well.

(iii) Prayer demands *submission.* One of the most striking features of Christ's earthly life is His submission to the Father. This characteristic continues from His first recorded word, 'I must be about My Father's business,' right through to His Garden prayer, 'nevertheless, not as I will, but as You will' (Luke 2:49; Matt. 26:39).

Christ's example teaches us that effective prayer requires submission to God. In 'The Learner's Prayer' He teaches us to pray, 'Your kingdom come. Your will be done on earth as it is in heaven' (Matt. 6:10). It is God's will, not our own, which is to be done and prayer which expresses only our own desires defies its very nature and defeats its purpose.

At times we are all guilty of 'offering prayers which we are not *willing* to have answered'.[16] When this is the case we are only addressing words to God, not praying! In *The Still Hour,* Austin Phelps asks, 'Are you living for the things you are praying for?' 'What one thing are you doing for Christ which costs you self-denial?' 'Are you *seeking* for opportunities to deny yourself, to save souls?' 'Are you willing to be *like* Him who had not where to lay His head?'[17]

When we pray, 'Your will be done', it is not an escape clause releasing us from specific expectation in prayer. Rather it is the affirmation of our submission to our Father. By so praying we acknowledge that His will is always best and we always desire that it be done. Apart from submission intercession can never be accomplished. For the position of true intercession is our submission, as we bow before the Lord.

(iv) Prayer is *intercession for others.* Prayer is more than intercession, but from Christ's example we know that this is one of its main functions. 'We are never more like Christ than in prayers of intercession. In the most lofty devotion we become unconscious of self.'[18] For whom do we intercede in our prayers? Is our tendency to pray only, or most often, for ourselves and those close to us? If so, this may indicate the smallness and selfishness of our prayer life. This is not the way Christ prayed. Paul wrote that 'supplications, prayers, intercession, and giving of thanks be made for all men' (1 Tim. 2:1). This characterized Christ's praying, and as we pray after His example we are to 'Bear one another's burdens, and so fulfill the law of Christ' (Gal. 6:2).

Christ's intercession was predicted by Isaiah: 'He was numbered with the transgressors, and He bore the sin of many, and made intercession for the transgressors' (53:12). Intercession takes place when we involve ourselves in the needs of others. Sometimes, as in Christ's case, this is to the extent that our own needs are set aside, or even forgotten. Revealed in His prayers are many for whom He made intercession. Among them are the following: (i) Luke 22:31,32, Peter, that his faith would remain strong in temptation; (ii) Luke 6:12,13; John 17:6-26, His disciples, and all, including ourselves, who will believe on Him; (iii) Mark 10:16, Little children, those whom concerned parents brought to Him. In a dark age as ours how great should be our inter-cession for such little ones! (iv) Matthew 5:44; Luke 23:34, His enemies, those who rejected Him, placing Him on the cross. How startling must His prayer from the cross have been, 'Father, forgive them,' And how it must have stirred many to consider Him afresh.

These are specific examples of Christ's intercession. Yet, in a wider sense, 'Every prayer of Christ was intercession because He had given Himself for us. All He asked and received was in our interest; every prayer He prayed was in the spirit of self-sacrifice.'[19] Intercession marked Christ's earthly prayer ministry and it extends beyond into heaven. What a heart-warming truth it is to know that

'He is also able to save to the uttermost those who come to God through Him, since He ever lives to make intercession for them' (Heb. 7:25).

(v) Effective prayer is often characterized by *solitude*. In reading and re-reading the Gospels focusing on Christ's teaching and practice of prayer one feature frequently appears. He often withdrew to some solitary place to pray. Several examples of this custom serve to stress its importance:

(i) Mark 1:35, He arose a long while before dawn and went to a solitary place to pray;

(ii) Mark 6:46, After feeding the 5,000 He sent the disciples away and went to a mountain to pray alone;

(iii) Luke 5:16, Following the healing of a leper and the press of people who came to hear and be healed by Him, He went into the wilderness to pray;

(iv) Luke 6:12, Prior to the calling of the Twelve He spent the night praying alone on a mountain;

(v) Luke 22:39-46, In the Garden Peter, John and James accompanied Him only so far, then He went on alone to pray.

(vi) Luke 23:34,46; Matthew 27:46; Mark 15:34, Christ's prayers from the Cross reveal a level of aloneness beyond that ever experienced by us. His isolation there was complete, as He was separated even from His Father.

A favourite verse of mine is Psalm 46:10, 'Be still and know that I am God'. Stillness is best achieved in solitude, when we separate ourselves from others to be with God in a special way. In such a position His priorities and perspectives come more easily into focus. Perhaps this is why Christ urged His disciples to 'Come aside by yourselves to a deserted place and rest awhile' (Mark 6:31). He wanted them to rest from the rush of life, to refresh themselves with God, to be prepared in solitude to better serve in society.

Part of prayer is being still and alone with God. This is something which may be accomplished on a mountain, in a desert, or in a quiet room in our own home. Yet, 'No one seems to want (and no one can find) a place for quiet - because, when you are quiet you have to face reality'.[20] And reality is about the last thing anyone wants to face today! It is a puzzling phenomenon of our age that even while walking in the hills above our home I find people wearing personal stereo headsets. Thus, even there they ensure that reality is eluded, silence banned and their thoughts are not their own. A. W. Tozer has observed that 'Civilization is so complex as to make the devotional life all but impossible. It wears us out by multiplying distractions and beats us down by destroying our solitude, when otherwise we might drink and renew our strength before going out to face the world'.[21] If our attitude toward solitude is any indication, it would seem we are far more willing to face the world than to be alone with ourselves or God. And yet, Christ went often to isolated places for prayer. He sought and found mountain retreats and desert quiet even when others were seeking Him. And there He prayed, and in this too He is our pattern.

'It has been said that no great work in literature or in science was ever wrought by a man who did not love solitude. We may lay it down as an elemental principle of religion, that no large growth in holiness was ever gained by one who did not take time to be often long alone with God.'[22]

(vi) Effective prayer includes *silence.* One of the benefits of solitude is silence. Generally we consider prayer to be verbal, words spoken, or thoughts ordered in the form of words. This is not all there is to prayer for it is also listening. The 'still small voice' may seldom be heard because we are seldom silent to hear it. Christ said, 'My sheep hear My voice, and I know them and they follow Me' (John 10:27). Can we follow Him without hearing Him? It is true that we may hear Him in Scripture, but is this the only way? May we not also hear Him as we wait before Him in silent expectation? He will not give us a new message in our quiet place. Nor will He go against or beyond His revealed Word in Scripture. But He will affirm His Word to us, open it in freshness before us and fill our waiting souls with Himself. Prayer is two-directional, we speak to God and He speaks to us. It is a sad characteristic of contemporary religion that many desire dialogue with everyone else, yet only engage in monologue with God.

Christ said, 'He who has sent Me is true; and I speak to the world those things which I have heard from Him' (John 8:26). In prayer, we too can hear from God if we will listen. And to listen is important, 'We are to put everything second so we can be alive to the voice of God and allow it to speak to us and confront us.'[23]

In one of the Servant Sections of Isaiah's prophecy we find these words which speak of Christ. 'The Lord God has given Me the tongue of the learned, That I should know how to speak a word in season to him who is weary. He awakens Me morning by morning. He awakens My ear to hear as the learned' (Isa. 50:4).

What is more important than hearing from God? A good prayer for us to pray is that we too might have an 'ear to hear as the learned'. To do so is to further conform to Christ's likeness.

References

1. David Icke, *The Truth Vibrations* (London: The Aquarian Press, 1991), pp. 136-139.

2. Michael Cole, Tony Higton, Jim Graham, David C. Lewis, *What Is The New Age?* (London: Hodder and Stoughton, 1990), p. 7.

3. Paul Kurtz, editor, *The Humanist Manifestos*, I And II (Buffalo, New York: Prometheus Books, 1973), p. 9.

4. D. Martyn Lloyd-Jones, *Studies In The Sermon On The Mount*, Vol I (Grand Rapids: Wm. B. Eerdmans Publishing Company, 1959), p. 45.

5. James S. Stewart, *The Life And Teaching Of Jesus Christ* (Edinburgh: The Church of Scotland Committee on Youth, 1933), p. 103.

6. D. Martyn Lloyd-Jones, *Studies In The Sermon On The Mount*, Vol II (Grand Rapids: Wm. B. Eerdmans Publishing Company, 1959), p. 50.

7. Austin Phelps, *The Still Hour* (Edinburgh: The Banner of Truth Trust, 1974), p31.

8. F. W. Krummacher, *The Suffering Saviour* (Chicago: Moody Press, n.d.), p. 67.

9. David M. McIntyre, *The Prayer-Life of Our Lord* (London: Marshal, Morgan and Scott Ltd., n.d.), p. 93.

10. Warren W. Wiersbe, *Prayer Basic Training* (Amersham-On-The-Hill, England: Scripture Press, 1982), p. 17.

11. G. Campbell Morgan, *The Practice of Prayer* (Grand Rapids: Baker Book House, 1971), p. 58.

12. E. M. Bounds, *Power Through Prayer* (Grand Rapids: Zondervan Publishing House, 1975), p. 36.

13. A. W. Tozer, *The Best of Tozer* (Eastbourne, England: Kingsway Publications, 1983), p. 39.

14. Baron Friedrich von Hugel, *Selected Letters 1896-1924*, editor, Bernard Holland (New York: E. P. Dutton and Co., 1933), p. 147.

15. *Hymns of Faith* (London: Scripture Union, 1975) no. 444.

16. Phelps, op cit, p. 19.

17. *Ibid.*, p. 23.

18. *Ibid.*, p. 80.

19. Andrew Murray, *Like Christ* (Three Hills, Alberta, Canada: Prairie Press, n.d.), p. 118.

20. Francis A. Schaeffer, *No Little People* (Downers Grove, IL: InterVarsity Press, 1974), p. 86.

21. A. W. Tozer, *Of God And Men* (Harrisonburg, PA: Christian Publications, Inc., 1960), p. 103.

22. Phelps, op cit, p. 64

23. Schaeffer, *op cit*, pp. 86,87.

The cross of Christ is man's only glory or it is his final stumbling-block.

Samuel M. Zwemer

For the sake of Jesus we have taken up this cross; for Jesus' sake let us persevere in the cross. He will be our Helper, who is our Captain and our Forerunner. Behold in the cross is all, and all depends upon our dying; and there is no other way to life, and to true inward peace, but the way of the holy cross, and of daily mortification.

Thomas a Kempis

If anyone desires to come after Me, let him deny himself, and take up his cross, and follow Me.　　　Matthew 16:24

We must do something about the cross, and one of two things only we can do - flee it or die upon it.

A. W. Tozer

Any believer can avoid the cross simply by being conformed to the world and its ways.

William MacDonald

You do not understand Christ till you understand his cross.

P. T. Forsyth

For I determined not to know anything among you except Jesus Christ and Him crucified.

1 Corinthians 2:2

But God forbid that I should glory except in the cross of our Lord Jesus Christ, by whom the world has been crucified to me, and I to the world.

Galatians 6:14

8

THE TWO CROSSES

In this chapter we come to a consideration of the cross of Jesus Christ and its meaning for the Christian. To those of us who have received Christ as Saviour His cross means many things. It is a paradox: the symbol both of death and life. It is an enigma: the essence of its meaning being immediately understood by a child, yet the oldest believer never succeeding in probing its fullest depths. Sometimes it evokes the deepest sadness. Other times it elicits the most exultant hymns of joy. The cross of Christ is the emblem of grace and reconciliation such as no other religion has, for only the Christian God has provided Himself as a substitute to bear the condemnation of man's sin. Only He has given us Himself, and thus offered the free gift of forgiveness and life in His presence.

Not all men see the cross as the Christian does. Paul begins 1 Corinthians 1:18 by saying, 'For the message of the cross is foolishness to those who are perishing ...' Those who were perishing in the first century considered it foolish and those of every successive generation continue to view it in the same way. The cross is the only way God has provided for man to come to Himself, yet men always seek an alternative which seem more credible to them. The cross condemns us and our best efforts to please God. It reveals our sin and exposes our inability to help ourselves. The alternatives men devise are designed to save their pride as well as their soul. Of course Satan is always willing to encourage such deception as it

171

serves his purpose admirably. Throughout the ages human alternatives to the cross have taken many forms, often being offered in the guise of religion.

Prominent in our day is the pseudo-religious alternative put forward by the New Age Movement. This Movement emphasises the presumed higher nature of mankind. The cross says we cannot save ourselves. The New Age Movement says we can. The cross begins with God and His love. The New Age Movement begins with man and his ability. The cross gives all the glory in salvation to God. The New Age Movement rests all its hope in humanity, assuming the supreme value and self-perfection of our own nature. The glory is man's in his self-salvation. To those who accept New Age teaching the message of Christ's cross seems irrelevant and foolish. There is no need for a Substitute to die for us on the cross if we are capable of saving ourselves.

As I write this chapter the influence of the New Age Movement is spreading throughout the Western world and beyond. And at the same time Islam is moving westward with formidable purpose, often increasing where Christianity is in decline. In Islam, as in the New Age Movement, there is no place for the cross of Christ.

Those who worship Allah generally hold one of two basic views of the cross. (i) The traditional Muslim view is that 'Jesus was not crucified at all. Instead someone else was crucified: some suggest Judas Iscariot. Jesus was safely carried away by angels to heaven and so was never crucified'.[1]   (ii) An alternative view is accepted by Ahmediyya Muslims who 'teach that Jesus *was* crucified, but did not die on the cross. Instead he only appeared to die, but Nicodemus ... and Joseph revived him in the cool of the tomb. After his recovery Jesus is supposed to have gone to India and to have died in Kashmir'.[2]

Belief in either of these views involves rejection of the cross of Christ and its message for mankind. As these two major contemporary religious movements suggest, in our day the cross is considered foolish by many. There is more to what Paul writes in 1 Corinthians 1:18. Not only does he say that 'the message of the cross is foolishness to those who are perishing', but he adds that 'to those who are being saved it is the power of God'. It has always been, and continues to be the power of God for man's salvation regardless of religious trends or human rejection. It is God's power and His power will always prevail.

If the cross is to have its proper place in our generation we who are Christians must proclaim it. Its message must be the heart of our ministry and we must deny ourselves, place our feet in the prints left by our Lord, take up our own cross and follow Him (Matt. 16:24). For not only must the cross be proclaimed, but it must also be applied. It is the emblem of both death and life, of an ending and a new beginning.

The Cross is Central to Christianity

The cross is the heart of the Gospel and the Gospel in its essence is Jesus Christ. In Galatians 6:14 Paul states the view of the cross which should be held by every believer: 'But God forbid that I should glory except in the cross of our Lord Jesus Christ, by whom the world has been crucified to me, and I to the world.' It was *on* the cross that Christ was crucified and it is *in* Christ that the believer is crucified. Both He, and we who receive Him, died on the cross. And as He lives on this side of His cross, so we are to live on this side of the cross as well. Our spiritual life begins with death, Christ's and ours, and our new life which flows from Christ through death is to be lived by His power and in His likeness. The error of much of contemporary Christianity is that the cross is seen only as the symbol of death and not of life. We must come to Christ's cross to receive new life. We must then go on from His cross bearing our own cross, characterized by daily dying to self and the world and a living conformity to the Risen Saviour.

There is no New Testament event comparable to that of the cross. The amount of space given to the final week of Christ's earthly life makes up about one third to one half of each of the Gospels. They focus on His death as they do on no other aspect of His life. This is so because the cross is central to Christ and Christianity. We can never understand Christ apart from His cross. It was His predetermined goal. It was the reason for the days of His flesh. And 'if the Cross of Christ is anything to the mind, it is surely everything - the most profound reality and the sublimest mystery. One comes to realize that literally all the wealth and glory of the gospel centres here'.[3]

The cross is crucial to God's plan for man's redemption for by it the dilemma of sin is resolved. God is holy, therefore He cannot simply ignore our sin. He is also love, therefore He does not desire that we receive the judgment we deserve as the consequence of our sin. As we are unable to help ourselves, He put Himself in our place, and the just anger and judgment incurred by our sin is diverted by His cross. There the Christ of God bore our sin in His own body (1 Peter 2:24). There the despised Man of Sorrows bore our griefs, carried our sorrows and was stricken and smitten by God for our transgressions (Isa. 53:3-5). In Him, we who cannot heal ourselves, are healed; our souls being made whole and holy by His blood. We should consider carefully the cross of Christ. Salvation is free only to those who receive it. It was gained by the Giver at great cost.

Crucifixion
When the Gospel writers speak of Christ's death each one says simply that 'they crucified Him' (Matt. 27:35; Mark 15:24; Luke 23:33; John 19:18).

In the first century world, both Jew and Gentile held a despised view of this torturous death and those who died by it. The Jewish view of crucifixion is summarised in a single sentence carried from the Old Testament into the New: 'Cursed is everyone who hangs on a tree' (Deut. 21:23; Gal. 3:13). And the Roman Cicero, representative of all Gentiles, calls it the 'cruelest, most hideous of punishments', and pleads that it may never 'come near the bodies of Roman citizens, never near their thoughts or eyes or ears'.[5]

Yet in each of the Gospels we read: 'they crucified Him'. The Jews did so because they thought Him guilty of the religious crime of blasphemy, claiming equality with God. The Romans, concerned about their power and position in Jewish Palestine, put Him to death for the political crime of sedition. They saw Him as an insurrectionist, a threat to the authority of Rome. These are the reasons for Christ's crucifixion given in history. But in reality it was human sin that hammered Him to the cross, and it was Divine love that held Him there. Crucifixion was a horrible way to die. Yet it was toward this death that Christ set His face like a flint (Isa. 50:7). This was the reason behind His humility and condescension, His coming as one of us to be crucified for us (Phil 2:8).

Two Deaths

In the New Testament we discover two deaths which are integral to Christianity. Between them they reveal the way of salvation and the nature of the life salvation secures. One death is Christ's - the other ours. If we are to live in Christ and He in us, we must first die with Him. This is the basis of the true Christian life. He came to die, and if we are to live following His example, we too must die. There was no other way for Him to save us and apart from our death in Him, there is no other way for us to be saved. His death made eternal life possible and our death by faith in Him makes it personal. Salvation for Christ and the sinner means death. To those who are perishing death sounds final, but to those who are being saved it sounds a triumphal note of hope and a new beginning.

Everything in Christ's life centred in His death. The three great events which divide His time on earth were: His birth, His death and His resurrection. Central to these is His death on the cross. In considering each of these we find the first, Christ's birth, to have been a quiet affair. Weary travellers Joseph and Mary, arriving finally at their destination, no matter that it was humble Bethlehem's stable. There Jesus was born, an event both mysterious and miraculous which has changed the world. Yet it was witnessed by only those involved. The shepherds came later, the wise men even later still. There were no multitudes to behold the intimate process of God being born in human form.

Christ's resurrection was much the same as His birth. We know of no one who witnessed the rolling away of the stone revealing the empty tomb. We know of no one who saw Christ emerge from the regions of death. Many saw Him afterward in His post-resurrection appearances, but no human eye beheld Him as He stepped from death into life again.

In this regard His death was entirely different from either His birth or resurrection. The cross was public, it was a spectacle. Many saw Him as He hung upon the cross in the agony of its death. His mother was there, John the Apostle, the soldiers, chief priests, scribes, elders, a varied multitude assembled to witness His death. Those who gathered were family, friends, His enemies, those who knew Him well and loved Him, those who hated Him and those who simply were curious. They all came and they all saw Him on His cross. There has never been such a public spectacle in all of history. Of Christ's birth, death and resurrection, it was His death which was beheld by the watching world. On His cross Christ was on display before the world.

Two Crosses

As there are two deaths integral to the Christian message, so there are two crosses as well. One is Christ's, the other ours. In each of the Synoptic Gospels Christ speaks of the believer's cross (Matt. 16:24,25; Mark 8:34,35; Luke 9:23,24). He says, 'If anyone desires to come after Me, let him deny himself and take up his cross daily, and follow Me. For whoever desires to save his life will lose it, but whoever loses his life for My sake will save it' (Luke 9:23,24). The believer's cross is the cross of true discipleship. It is personal, we must each bear our own cross daily in self-denial. This is a biblical truth seldom taught today and perhaps even more rarely applied in the lives of those who consider themselves followers of Christ.

I remember some years ago sitting in a graduate seminar in Chicago. We were discussing the application of biblical Christianity in a practical sense and the professor posed a question: 'How many of you have ever heard or preached a message on the believer's cross?' There were about 18 of us present, from a dozen different countries around the world. In response to this question I was the only one who could raise a hand. Perhaps this group was an exception, but it does not seem likely. Since then I have listened carefully for this message and have heard it only on the rarest occasions.

The believer's cross means self-denial. To preach self-denial is to preach an unpopular message. Today we are more interested in self-affirmation and self-realization than we are in self-denial. As there are many who reject Christ's cross through disbelief, there are many it seems, who believe in His cross, yet reject their own. The cross in Scripture is two-fold, Christ's and ours. Both are essential, the first for spiritual life, the second for abundant life. The message of the cross cuts across the casualness of much of contemporary Christianity and calls us again to Golgotha. The cross means death. It meant death for Christ and it means the death of our old nature, death to the world for all who would follow Christ.

I do not believe this has been more plainly stated than it is by A. W. Tozer in his essay, *The Old Cross and the New*. Tozer observes that the new cross of much popular religion does not mean death but redirection. It saves the sinners self-respect, but not his soul.

'The old cross is a symbol of death. It stands for the abrupt, violent end of a human being. The man in Roman times who took up his cross and started down the road had already said good-bye to his friends. He was not coming back. He was going out to have it ended. The cross made no compromise, modified nothing, spared nothing; it slew all of the man, completely and for good. It did not try to keep on good terms with its victim. It struck cruel and hard, and when it had finished its work, the man was no more ... God salvages the individual by liquidating him and then raising him again to newness of life ... God offers life, but not an improved life. The life He offers is life out of death. It stands always on the far side of the cross.'[5]

The Cross Means Sacrifice

Christ's death on the cross was the culmination of all the Old Testament sacrificial system. It was what every offering on the Day of Atonement anticipated. It was the reality of which they were only the shadow (Heb. 10:1). All of the annual Jewish sacrifices served only as a 'reminder of sins every year. For it is not possible that the blood of bulls and goats could take away sins' (Heb. 10:3,4).

But when Christ came He was the fulfilment of every Old Testament prophecy concerning the Messiah, and by His coming He brought an end forever to the sacrificial system for He 'offered one sacrifice for sins forever', and having done so, 'He sat down at the right hand of God' (Heb. 10:12). Christ's sacrifice on the cross of Calvary was the last sacrifice but one! His cross marked the end of God's demand for sacrifice with a single exception! The last sacrifice is ours and is made possible by His.

In Romans 12:1,2 Paul writes about this sacrifice which is linked to the believer's cross: 'I beseech you therefore, brethren, by the mercies of God that you present your bodies a living sacrifice, holy, acceptable to God, which is your reasonable service. And do not be conformed to this world, but be transformed by the renewing of your mind, that you may prove what is that good and acceptable and perfect will of God.'

The sacrifice Paul writes of is nothing like that made on the Old Testament Day of Atonement. Then a lamb was offered as a substitute, now the offering is to be ourselves. Then the lamb was to be perfect, now God receives us just as we are and will transform us by His power into the likeness of His Son. Then it was a lifeless form placed upon a stone altar, now it is a 'living sacrifice', characterized by daily dying to self and the world. Then the offering was made in obedience to the demand of the law, now it is in response to the invitation of grace. Paul beseeches each of us to make this offering on the basis of all of Christ's mercies completed on Calvary. This is the last sacrifice, and it is ours. As Christ's cross contained His sacrifice, so ours does as well. There cannot be one without the other. Christ made Himself a sacrifice for us. We are the reason He had a cross at all. Now we are to give ourselves as living sacrifices and carry our crosses for Him. This is the application of the message of the cross.

In his book, *The Cross of Christ*, John Stott writes that the purpose of Christ's 'self-giving on the cross was not just to save isolated individuals, and so to perpetuate their loneliness, but to create a new community whose members would belong to him, love one another and eagerly serve the world ... the community of Christ is the community of the cross. Having been brought into being by the cross, it continues to live by and under the cross. Our perspective and our behaviour are now governed by the cross. All our relationships have been radically transformed by it ... In particular the cross revolutionizes our attitudes to God, to ourselves, to other people both inside and outside the Christian fellowship ...'[6] It is as we deny ourselves and sacrificially serve God and others that the message of His cross is applied as we bear our own cross.

To become part of the 'community of the cross' we must not only come to it for salvation, but go forward from it for service. We must continually sacrifice self, saying 'no' to our own will and 'yes' to His. It is just as Thomas a Kempis wrote so long ago.

> 'Behold in the cross is all, and all depends upon our dying' and there is no other way to life, and to true inward peace, but the way of the holy cross, and of daily mortification ... Know for certain that thou must lead a dying life; and the more a man dies to himself, the more he begins to live to God.'[7]

References

1. Peter Cottrell, *Why do Muslims say that Jesus did not die on the cross?* (Evangelical Times, February 1986) p. 2.

2. *Ibid.* Note: The Koran, Sura 4:157, says that 'They slew him not and they crucified him not, but they had only his likeness... they did not really slay him, but God took him up to himself." Also, Sura 6:164, which teaches that no one can take another's punishment, thus denying the substitutionary work of Christ on man's behalf.

3. John Stott, *The Cross of Christ* (Leicester: Inter-Varsity Press, 1986), p. 41.

4. James S. Stewart, *The Life And Teaching of Jesus Christ* (Edinburgh: The Church of Scotland Committee on the Religious Instruction of Youth, 1965), p. 179.

5. A. W. Tozer, *The Best of Tozer* (Eastbourne: Kingsway Publishers, 1983), pp. 175-177.

6. Stott. *op cit*, pp. 255,256.

7. Thomas A Kempis, *The Imitation of Christ* (London: Samuel Bagster And Sons, Third Edition, n.d.), pp. 82, 87.

Gentlemen, it would be easy to start a new religion to compete with Christianity. All the founder would have to do is die and then be raised from the dead.

Voltaire

But now Christ is risen from the dead, and has become the firstfruits of those who have fallen asleep.

I Corinthians 15:20

No man saw Jesus rise from the dead; only a few saw him risen; but all men are affected by his resurrection in one way or another.

Everett Harrison

Your dead shall live; Together with my dead body they shall arise. Awake and sing, you who dwell in dust; For your dew is like the dew of herbs, And the earth shall cast out the dead.

Isaiah 26:19

If the story is true, then a wholly new mode of being has risen in the universe.

C. S. Lewis

He who would preach the gospel must go directly to preaching the resurrection of Christ. He who does not preach the resurrection is no apostle, for this is the chief part of our faith ... Everything depends on our retaining a firm hold on this article (of faith) in particular; for if this one totters and no longer counts, all the others will lose their value and validity.

Martin Luther

If then you were raised with Christ, seek those things which are above, where Christ is, sitting at the right hand of God. Set your mind on things above, not on things on the earth.

Colossians 3:1-2

THE RESURRECTION

'One short sleep past,
We wake eternally,
And death shall be no more,
Death thou shalt die.'[1]

'Death is swallowed up in victory. O Death, where is your sting?
O Hades, where is your victory' (1 Cor. 15:54,55)? The death of
death, an astonishing concept whether presented in the form of
poetry or Scripture. Is it possible that there could be an end of
death, rather than that death is the end of all things itself? Such
questions have stirred the minds of men from the beginning of time.

When the Apostle Paul preached to the Athenians assembled on
Mars Hill it was this doctrine that brought a reaction, 'When they
heard of the resurrection of the dead, some mocked, while others
said, We will hear you again on this matter' (Acts 17:32). It was this
doctrine also which troubled the Corinthian Church as some
denied its possibility, saying, 'There is no resurrection of the dead'
(1 Cor. 15:12). And when Paul was brought before King Agrippa
in Caesarea, in the midst of his testimony he asked the king a
question. 'Why should it be thought incredible by you that God
raises the dead' (Acts 26:8)? We aren't told what prompted Paul's
question, nor are we given the king's reply, but it was the resurrection of the dead that divided men then as now. Agrippa thought it

incredible, and he was correct. Yet, given the nature of God it would have been even more incredible had He *not* raised Christ from the dead. And it would be far more incredible if Christ did not resurrect those for whom He is the 'firstfruits' of the resurrection.

Because of God's plan and by His power it was not possible that the grave should hold His Son and it is no more possible that it should hold those for whom He died. This certainty is expressed from the beginning of biblical revelation. 3,000 years ago Job wrote, 'If a man dies, shall he live again? All the days of my hard service I will wait, till my change comes. You shall call, and I will answer You, You shall desire the work of Your hands' (Job 14:14,15). It is this certainty which is visualized in the New Testament account of Lazarus' resurrection. As Christ stood at the entrance of the tomb in Bethany He 'cried with a loud voice, Lazarus, come forth', and he did! (John 11:43,44) Death did not hold Christ; it will not hold those whom He calls.

By His resurrection Christ is 'declared to be the Son of God with power' (Rom. 1:4) God has 'loosed the pains of death' and 'Death is swallowed up in victory' (Acts 2:24; 1 Cor. 15:54) and the believer is made alive to 'a living hope ... to an inheritance incorruptible and un-defiled and that does not fade away, reserved in heaven' (1 Pet. 1:3,4).

Even as the believer is living in this future hope, the resurrection offers present help. Paul wanted to know its power in his life, and much of his spiritual success stems from having found the object of his desire. The resurrection influences not only the end of life's experience, but all of life. Its power is to be applied in our daily living and shown in our increasing conformity to the Son of God.

Because of its importance the resurrection has continually been the target of attack. Through the centuries various explanations have been offered to account for the empty garden tomb in order to avoid the literal bodily resurrection of Christ. In general they are variations of these basic theories.

(i) *The Theft Theory* suggests that Christ's body was stolen by the disciples, Joseph of Arimathaea, or even a grave robber drawn to the tomb by the public nature of Christ's death.

(ii) *The Swoon Theory* suggests that there was no death and thus no need for a resurrection. This is an aspect of Islamic as well as liberal theological teaching and implies that Christ became unconscious on the cross and then recovered in the cool of the tomb, perhaps aided by a sympathetic follower.

(iii) *The Vision Theory* suggests that Christ did die and remain dead. There was no literal bodily resurrection. Rather it was all psychological, an hallucination formed in the minds of His followers arising from their deep belief in His passion. They wanted Him to return to life and the strength of their desire caused them to see what was not there, to visualise the resurrected Christ they wanted to see.

Anyone wishing an alternative to Christ's real resurrection will find a variety readily available. My purpose in this chapter is not to show the error of such alternatives, but to consider the meaning of Christ's resurrection as it applies to those who have received Him as Saviour. For me His literal resurrection is an established fact, historically and biblically verifiable. It is a truth made personal by experience. Christ has risen; He is alive! But what difference does it make to we who are living at the close of the 20th century that He rose from the dead toward the beginning of the 1st century?

The significance of the resurrection is the subject Paul addresses in First Corinthians 15. Here he leaves no doubt as to its importance as he points out the following:

(i) v 13, 'But if there is no resurrection of the dead, then Christ is not risen';

(ii) v 14, 'And if Christ is not risen, then our preaching is vain and your faith is also vain';

(iii) v 17, 'And if Christ is not risen, your faith is futile; you are still in your sins!

(iv) v 19, 'If in this life only we have hope in Christ, we are of all men the most pitiable.'

It was this doctrine which lay at the heart of the sermons preached from Pentecost onward in the book of Acts. It was the completion of the Gospel good news; the truth without which there could be no Gospel message at all.

When Jesus rose from the dead 'He forced open a door that had been locked since the death of the first man. He has met, fought, and beaten the King of Death. Everything is different because He has done so. This is the beginning of a New Creation: a new chapter in cosmic history is opened'.[2] It is in this new chapter that the story of our eternal life is recorded. Because He lives we live in a totally new way in time, and will live forever in eternity.

Jesus was born to die, but He died in order to rise again and share with us His victory and give to us His power. Power not only to rise again, but to live in the glory of the resurrection in the present. 'Thanks be to God for His indescribable gift' (2 Cor. 9:15), and 'Thanks be to God who gives us the victory through our Lord Jesus Christ' (1 Cor. 15:57). It is because of this victory that we are to be 'Steadfast, immovable, always abounding in the work of the Lord' (1 Cor. 15:58).

The Resurrection of Christ

Before we consider the meaning of the resurrection as it relates to ourselves we will first look at it from Christ's perspective. What did it mean to Him? There are at least four great truths affirmed by His return to life from death.

(i) Romans 1:4. By His resurrection His Sonship is declared with power. All His claims of equality with the Father are vindicated. He is Truth and has spoken the truth even concerning this most awesome claim.

(ii) Romans 4:25. By His resurrection His Saviourhood is declared. He was 'delivered up because of our offences, and was raised because of our justification'. Had He remained in the grave we would have remained forever in our sins.

(iii) Romans 14:8,9. By His resurrection His Lordship is declared. 'For if we live, we live to the Lord; and if we die, we die to the Lord. That, whether we live or we die, we are the Lord's. For to this end Christ died and rose and lived again, that He might be Lord of both the dead and the living.' In life or death we are not our own, but Christ's. He has lived - died - resurrected - and lives again to affirm His sovereign rule over all and for all of time and eternity.

(iv) Romans 8:34. By His resurrection He enters into His present ministry as Intercessor on our behalf. 'It is Christ who has died, and furthermore is also risen, who is ever at the right hand of God, who also makes intercession for us.' Intercession is part of His heavenly activity. Its benefits, along with those of His Sonship, Saviourhood and Lordship, are directed toward the believer as we will see in the following sections.

The Resurrection of the Believer
The resurrection applies to the believer in a two-fold way. Generally we consider it in its future application. Following death, according to God's promise and Christ's example, we will be resurrected. Then our body will be reunited with our soul and we will be fully conformed to Christ Jesus with whom we will spend eternity. As the 'firstfruits' of the resurrection Christ assures us of our own resurrection similar to His - He returned to life in a literal and bodily way, so shall we. As He was raised never again to die, unlike Lazarus and the others resurrected in Scripture, so shall we be. This is the 'living hope' Peter speaks of (1 Pet. 1:3).

As incredible as this is, yet there is more to the resurrection. A second, and equally important aspect, applies to the present. It is the resurrection *in* life *before* we die. It is this feature of Christ's resurrection which should define the nature of the life we live as His followers on earth. Through God's power displayed in Christ's resurrection death is eternally defeated and it is by this same power that we may live our daily lives on this side of death. The greatest thing about Christ's resurrection is not what it says to us about death, but what it says to us about life. There is newness of life before and after death. In this sense the resurrection is an ongoing experience.

Writing of our future resurrection from death Paul says, 'We shall all be changed' (1 Cor. 15:51). But their is a change in the present as well as in the future. One of the greatest historical

185

evidences of Christ's resurrection is the immediate and profound change it produced in His disciples. Within 24 hours they were transformed totally and eternally. On the Saturday Christ spent in the confines of death the disciples seemed broken-hearted, His words 'My God, My God, why have You forsaken Me', ringing in their ears to despair. The hope, joy gone forever. The next day, the first Easter Sunday, as the reality of His return to life began to be confirmed the transformation began. We can only let our imagination race with the possibilities this news produced in them. He had died for them, now, because of His resurrection, they were willing to live and die for Him. Captivated by the truth and power of His resurrection they went out to turn their world upside down.

This doctrine has unique power to change lives. We may take Paul as an example. 'It gripped and mastered him, heart, mind, will, body, interests, friendships, habits, recreations - everything. It took him over, lock, stock and barrel, till he was a man utterly possessed. This is how he proved the power of the risen Christ in his life, bursting his bonds and driving him with a holy constraint across the ancient world, empowering him for service'.[3] And when this truth 'was believed in the 16th century, all Europe was set alight by the Reformers; it started a revolution, as everywhere men were raised to newness of life'.[4]

Christ Jesus was delivered up because of our offences, and was raised because of our justification' (Rom. 4:25). A justified man is a new man and 'Just as Christ was raised from the dead by the glory of the Father, even so we shall walk in newness of life' (Rom. 6:4). It is not just *awareness* of this newness, but *application* of this newness, which is possible, yet often lacking in our Christian lives today.

In Colossians 3:1-11 Paul describes the kind of people we can be - and should be, because of the resurrection.

'If then you were raised with Christ, seek those things which are above, where Christ is, sitting at the right hand of God. Set your mind on things above, not on things on the earth. For you died, and your life is hidden with Christ in God. When Christ who is our life appears, then we also will appear with Him in glory. Therefore put to death your members which are on the earth: fornication, uncleanness, passion, evil desire, and covetousness, which is idolatry. Because of these things the wrath of God is coming upon the sons of disobedience, in which you once walked when you lived in them. But now you must also put off all these: anger, wrath, malice, blasphemy, filthy language out of your mouth. Do not lie to one another, since you have put off the old man with his deeds, and have put on the new man who is renewed in knowledge according to the image of Him who created him, where there is neither Greek, nor Jew, circumcised nor uncircumcised, barbarian, Scythian, slave nor free, but Christ is all and in all.'

Christ's resurrection both produces this new life and provides the power by which it may be lived. It is because He is resurrected and ascended that the Holy Spirit has come to us and dwells in us (John 14:16,17; 16:7). Therein lies the power of the resurrection life. Paul makes this point plainly in Romans 8:11 affirming that it is the same Spirit who raised Jesus from the dead who dwells in us.

The Power of Christ's Resurrection
In Philippians 3:8-11 Paul expresses his deep desire to experience the power of Christ's resurrection in his own life. This passage unfolds as follows.

(i) v 8, For 'the excellence of the knowledge of Christ Jesus' Paul was willing to lose all. Already he had 'lost his status within Judaism, his reputation, and his opportunity for wealth and fame. He experienced ostracism, bodily harm, death threats, and property destruction (cf. Heb. 10:34). He may have forfeited his Jewish birthright and family inheritance'.[5] Yet, in order to 'gain Christ' he counted all this as nothing at all.

(ii) v 9, He had become righteous, not by the law, but 'through faith in Christ'. Willing to lose all he experienced gain; acceptance by God and a righteous standing before Him.

(iii) v 10, He was justified but he was not satisfied! Paul 'was a seeker and a finder and a seeker still'.[6] He wanted more than salvation - he wanted to know Christ and 'the power of His resurrection, and the fellowship of His sufferings, being conformed to His death'. His 'spirit was that of the loving explorer. He was a prospector among the hills of God searching for the gold of personal spiritual experience'.[7] Paul had been raised from the dust of the Damascus Road to walk in newness of life. Now he desired intimate knowledge of the One who raised him. And he desired the power of the resurrection to operate day by day in him. This power defeated death forever; he wanted it to defeat sin daily in his life.

In Ephesians 1:19-21 Paul prays a prayer for Divine power. He prays that we may know 'What is the exceeding greatness of His power toward us who believe, according to the working of His mighty power which He worked in Christ when He raised Him from the dead and seated Him at His right hand in the heavenly places, far above all principality and power and might and domin- ion, and every name that is named, not only in this age but also in that which is to come.'

Paul was willing to risk all because of the power of the resurrec- tion applied in his life. In our caution and conformity to the world, in our concern for the thoughts of others, there is often little room and less inclination for abandonment to God. Paul wished to give himself up to God so that the power of God might rise up in him to holy life and service.

In such a dark and depraved day as ours God calls us to live holy lives. Such a call may seem as impossible as walking on water. But Peter walked on the waves of Galilee so long as he beheld Christ. And 'We all, with unveiled face, beholding as in a mirror the glory of the Lord, are being transformed into the same image from glory to glory, just as by the Spirit of the Lord' (2 Cor. 3:18). By the Spirit's transformation comes our imitation of Christ. And as we yield to Him our conformity advances until our resurrection. Then, in the twinkling of an eye, the acceleration of our transfor- mation will make us 'like Him'.

References

1. John Donne, *The Poems of John Donne* ed. Sir Herbert Grieson (London: Oxford University Press, 1964), p. 297.

2. C .S. Lewis, *Miracles* (New York: The Macmillan Company, 1971), p. 150.

3. James Philip, *The Death and Resurrection of Christ* Sermon series preached at Holyrood Abbey, Edinburgh, (Dundee, Scotland: Geo. E. Findlay and Co. Ltd., n.d.), p. 79.

4. *Ibid.*, p. 78

5. Robert Gromacki, *Stand United in Joy* (Schaumburg, IL.: Regular Baptist Press, 1980), p. 145.

6. A. W. Tozer, *Keys to the Deeper Life* (Grand Rapids: Zondervan Publishing House, 1976), p. 25.

7. *Ibid.*

Also by

Christian Focus Publications

Jesus, Divine Messiah

Robert Reymond

The author takes eight descriptions of the Messiah found
in the Old Testament and shows how Jesus fulfilled each
one.

demy

ISBN 0 906 731 941   128 pages

The Root and Branch

Joseph Pipa

This book explores the mystery of Christ's two natures.
Its purpose is to enable us all to know the Saviour better.

B format

ISBN 1 871676 169   140 pages

The Person of Christ

Andrew Bonar

Bonar lived in daily fellowship with his Saviour and out of this rich experience describes what Jesus should mean to Christians today.

B format

ISBN 0 906731 836   128 pages

The Prayer Life of Jesus

David M McIntyre

Jesus is our prime example of how to develop meaningful prayer-lives. The author examines several Scripture references to Jesus' prayers and provides insight into how and when to pray.

pocket paperback

ISBN 1 85792 0104   160 pages

Behold Your God

Donald Macleod

A major work on the doctrine of God covering His power, anger, righteousness, name and being. This book will educate and stimulate to deeper thinking and worship.

demy

ISBN 1 871679 096   160 pages